History of the Sage and Slocum families of England and America

Including the allied families of Montague, Wanton, Brown, Josselyn, Standish, Doty, Carver, Jermain or Germain, Pierson, Howell. Hon. Russell Sage and Margaret Olivia (Slocum) Sage. The Slocum families showing three lines of descent from the signers of the Mayflower compact

Henry Whittemore

Alpha Editions

This edition published in 2019

ISBN : 9789353959333

Design and Setting By
Alpha Editions
email - alphaedis@gmail.com

History of the Sage and Slocum Families

Of England and America

Including the Allied Families of

Montague, Wanton, Brown, Josselyn, Standish, Doty, Carver, Jermain or Germain, Pierson, Howell

Hon. Russell Sage and Margaret Olivia (Slocum) Sage

The Slocum Families Showing
Three Lines of Descent

From the Signers of the Mayflower Compact

By Henry Whittemore
GENEALOGIST AND COMPILER OF FAMILY AND OTHER HISTORIES

New York 1908

Russell Sage

Introduction

Where one man achieves distinction in any line of business or profession there are ten thousand who fail, or reach only a moderate degree of success. The reason for this will be found by tracing the line of the individual to its original source and, though the line be followed for hundreds of years, even into the "dark ages," it will be found that certain characteristics are transmitted from generation to generation down to the present time. It will be found also that the allied families have exercised a potent influence in determining the character of the individual, although the chief characteristics of the original family usually predominate.

The History of the "Sage, Slocum and Allied Families" forms an interesting study in historical and genealogical research, showing, as it does, that in every generation, from the time of William the Conqueror down to the landing of the Pilgrims at Plymouth the principal family, or those of intermarriages in the direct line, have left their impress on each generation; and the descendants of these families of the Old World, chiefly of French and Saxon origin, inheriting the chief characteristics, have been largely instrumental in developing the resources of the New World. In the feudal ages representatives of these families were noted for their military prowess, and their high sense of honor; and on every battle-field of America for two hundred and fifty years, the names of Sage and Slocum are found inscribed on the rolls of honor. As lawyers, statesmen, educators, financiers, and promoters of American Industries they have all borne a conspicuous part; and among those who have distinguished themselves in the nineteenth and twentieth centuries there are few, if any, more worthy of remembrance than the descendants of these two families.

PART I.

THE SAGE AND ALLIED FAMILIES

THE SAGE AND ALLIED FAMILIES

HON. RUSSELL SAGE

His birth in the Empire State. His self-denying efforts to acquire an education. Early and successful business operations. A comparatively rich man at twenty-three. His political experience; the office sought the man. Elected Treasurer of the County. Defeated in his first nomination for Congress, and twice elected afterwards. His intimate friendship with President Zachary Taylor and U. S. Senator, William H. Seward. His remarkable record in Congress. His famous anti-slavery speech and his efforts to restore the Missouri Compromise. His record as Financier and Railroad Promoter, and his successful operations on Wall Street. Originator of the system of "Puts" and "Calls" and other well-known Wall Street methods.

AS merchant, statesman, financier and railroad promoter, Russell Sage stood among the foremost men of his time. His business and public career cover the most important period in the history of our country, and in all the great events of the half century of his activities he bore a conspicuous part. That he added millions to the wealth of the country, and aided materially in the development of its resources, none can deny; that in his business methods by which he accumulated his millions he made enemies is an accepted fact; and every successful man of business who keeps his own counsel and trusts to his own judgment necessarily makes enemies among narrow-minded imitative competitors, who fail to appreciate true genius, and measure every man by their own standard.

Mr. Sage was a man of the highest intellectual attainments, remarkable business sagacity, and almost prophetic in his far-seeing knowledge of the future as pertaining to present conditions. In every undertaking he saw the end from the beginning and laid his plans accordingly. "Insurmountable difficulties" had no terrors for him. Like Napoleon, when informed by his aids that the Alps stood between him and the enemy, replied: "Then there shall be no Alps!" If Mr. Sage, after due consideration found that the ends justified the means, he seldom failed to achieve his ends. Probably one of the greatest secrets of his success was the fact that he made few confidants. With a keen knowledge of human nature, he discussed his plans only with those whose friendship and discretion he had tested, and in whose integrity he knew he could confide. The business man, like the inventor, is justified in guarding well his own secrets; they are a part of his capital. Self-protection compels a man to fortify himself against the attacks of unscrupulous competitors, and Mr. Sage was no exception to this rule, but his methods were straight-forward, and no one ever accused him of dishonesty in his dealings. His strong sense of duty made him indifferent to public opinion. It would have been impossible for him to have become a politician according to the modern acception of the term, as he cared nothing for personal popularity. He was amenable only to that Higher Power which governed all his actions.

Hon. Russell Sage owed something to heredity, as the personal record of his American ancestors for seven generations clearly indicate, and these hereditary traits were manifest in every event of his life. The "image and superscription" of his forbears were stamped on every fibre of his nature; and he determined to make the most of his personality, either to repress or give full play in development, as circumstances might determine. He had just reason to feel proud of the achievements of his ancestors; they rendered important service to their country and this was the legacy they bequeathed to him and nothing more. They were hard working industrious men who made the most of their opportunities and their environment.

Hon. Russell Sage, son of Elisha and Prudence (Risley) Sage, (son of Elisha (2), son of Elisha (1), son of Amos, Son of Timothy, son of David), was born in Shenandoah, Verona township, Oneida County, New York, 4th of August, 1816, a year after the close of the second war between England and the United States. He just missed being born in the "land of steady habits;" and the Empire State, which has profited so much by his activities, can justly claim him as her own son, of which she has just reason to feel proud. This comparatively "Unknown Quantity" came on to the stage of existence just as the great industrial revolution of which he was to become a prominent factor began. The greatest discoveries, and the greatest advancement in civilization since the discovery of America, all occurred during his lifetime, and he became instrumental in the development of many of these, and lived to witness what appeared to be at the time of their inception, miraculous. He was but two years old when the first steam power press was set in motion in this or in any other country. The discovery of the first coal mines anti-dated his birth but ten years. The first gas was manufactured in the year of his birth. He was 13 years old when matches were placed on the market. At that time he was a salesman in a country store.

He was 14 years old when the first railroad was built in the United States, and cast his first vote before the first steamship crossed the ocean. He was nearly thirty years of age, and had already accumulated a fortune when Morse constructed his first telegraph line from Baltimore to Washington, and Edison was then "unknown."

The boy who little dreamed of the bewildering changes which were to take place became, before he died, one of the master spirits in the world of finance as well as of in any industrial and business enterprises. The boy to whom the railroad came as a marvel bordering on the miraculous, lived to become a heavy stockholder in a railroad mileage which would girdle the earth. No man ever lived who was a more active participant in changes so widespread and momentous as those which have been a part of the life of Russell Sage. The event which made the first great impression upon the boy was the building of the Erie Canal. The State authorized the construction of the waterway in the year of his birth, and the canal was completed when he was nine years old. It ran through Oneida County not far from the Sage farm.

"Whenever I had a chance," he was fond of saying in his later years, "I watched the men at work on it. Even as a child I had great faith in the enterprise and a clear idea of the route and subject. It was a red-letter day with me when they let the water into the ditch, and I watched it rise to the level."

Russell Sage virtually knew no childhood. When other boys of his age were pursuing the elementary branches of education, he was working out the great problems of life and planning for the future. "Boyhood," once mused Mr. Sage, when asked for his reminiscences of that period, "I don't suppose I ever had any. It was nothing but work. After I went into my brother's store, I realized that I was lacking in education and I determined to spend a part of my small earnings in attending night school. Of the $4.00 wages, I got on the first of every month, I paid $1.50 to my teacher. I soon learned book-keeping, and the more intricate problems in arithmetic. I managed to borrow some books on history and read all the papers I could get my hands on, I had no time for anything else."

At the end of a year his wages were increased $2.00 a month. When he was 13 years old he was making $4.00 a week. He saved almost every cent.

Across the street were two vacant lots which he made up his mind to own. They cost him $200.00 which had taken several years to save. In this period of his activities he was something of a horse trader. Horses, as in all new lands were in great demand, and there was no shrewder judge of horseflesh anywhere than the grocery clerk. He made more money with every deal and bought more land. He was still a clerk at this time with his brother, Henry Sage, of Troy.

With some of his profits he bought a sloop which he navigated from Troy to New York. He handled a lot of horses on commission and landed them safely in New York where he disposed of them to advantage, studied market conditions, and started home with a cargo of provisions. The trip netted him $700.00, and he quit his clerkship as soon as he reached home, entering into partnership in a new store with his brother, Elisha Montague Sage. In less than two years he was able to buy his brother out.

In 1839, the great temperance wave known as the "Washingtonian plan," swept over the country, and it was necessary to do away with the liquor end of the store. This reduced the profits of the business. He sold out at a good price, and found himself at the age of 22 with at least $25,000 in cash and owning several tracts of land with his staunch sloops as another asset.

In all the time he had sold liquor, when it was customary for nearly every one to drink, including Christians, and ministers of the gospel, he had never touched a drop himself. He had handled many a cigar and piece of tobacco across his counters, but he never smoked or chewed, and in that day chewing and smoking were considered as manly qualities, and any boy who could get through the initiatory process of sickness was looked up to by his playmates and companions. It is related of Mr. Sage that on one occasion he attempted a cigar. The sickness cured him, and he never tried tobacco again in any form.

Finding himself after having barely attained his majority with what was in those days considered a fortune, with inexpensive habits, and possessing great frugality in the matter of his expenditures, he cast about him for some new line of activity. It was but an advancement along natural lines that he should enter into the commission business with New York connections. In the course of a very short time the firm controlled several branches of trade not only in Troy, but in Albany.

As early as 1850 Mr. Sage branched out on broader lines in the transportation business. In 1853, as a member of the Troy Common Council, he took a leading part in the sale of the Troy and Schenectady Railroad, then owned by the city; and which now forms a part of the New York Central system. A little later he became a large owner in the Lacrosse Railroad, now the Chicago, Milwaukie and St. Paul.

Mr. Sage began his political career at a very early age, and, like everything else he undertook he was successful. He was elected to the Common Council of Troy in 1845. Later he was elected Treasurer of Rensselaer County, and held the position for seven years.

An incident occurred in 1847 that had an important bearing on Mr. Sage's political career. The occasion was a banquet where he met for the first time Gen. Zachary

Taylor, and the two became warm friends. Mr. Sage, at this time, publicly challenged the statement that the guest of honor, Gen. John A. Wood, was the real hero of Buena Vista. He contended that the real hero was General Zachary Taylor; and the ablest military critics and historians justify Mr. Sage's claim.

Mr. Sage, in 1848, was a delegate to the National Congress of the Whig party, and took a foremost part in nominating General Taylor for the Presidency, and the latter felt under deep obligations to him, and availed himself of the first opportunity to show his appreciation of Mr. Sage's efforts.

When General Taylor was elected President one of the problems he had to face was the rivalry between the anti and pro-slavery leaders. The situation caused considerable friction over the nominations made by Senator Seward for important New York offices, and Mr. Sage went to Washington in the Senator's behalf, his opponents in the meantime using every effort to defeat his political aspirations. The President had not forgotten the kindness of Mr. Sage, and he gladly made the appointments suggested by Mr. Seward.

Mr. Sage thus made a life-long friend of Senator Seward, and never neglected an opportunity to do him an act of kindness, or assist him in carrying out his policies and contributing to his political success. Mr. Sage formed strong friendships, which lasted through life. It was only those who knew him intimately that could appreciate his high moral worth and true nobility of character. What the public at large thought of him was a matter of little concern to him.

In 1850 Mr. Sage was nominated for Congress on the Whig ticket, but was defeated. Two years later, however, he was successful at the polls, and in 1854 was re-elected by an overwhelming majority. In Congress Mr. Sage proved himself one of the ablest debaters, and one of the strongest advocates of the principles of the Republican party, which were not then very popular. He supported the Kansas and Nebraska Bill and opposed the repeal of the Missouri Compromise, measures which exasperated the South, and helped to force the issue and led finally to the secession of several of the Southern States, thus precipitating the Civil War. Mr. Sage was fearless in proclaiming a doctrine he believed to be right; and any measure that tended to abridge the liberties of one section at the expense of the other he did not hesitate to firmly oppose, whatever might be the consequences.

The efforts of the Southern leaders and advocates of slavery to repeal the Missouri Compromise—after a solemn pledge entered into four years previous—which it was believed at the time would remove sectional animosities and restore peace and harmony throughout every part of the Union, called forth the noblest sentiments, the loftiest patriotism, and skilfull statesmanship of which Mr. Sage was capable. He had made an exhaustive study of the subject, and viewed it from every stand-point, and took the most charitable view possible for a man in his position, who felt that he had a solemn duty to perform regardless of the opinions of others. Mr. Sage was noted for his brevity, and this was probably the longest speech he ever prepared, and one of the longest made in Congress during that exciting period. It covered twenty pages of the *Congressional Globe*, of 2500 words to the page, aggregating some 17,000 words. He dealt only in facts, of which he had an abundant supply, and made no attempt at display. It was an honest, manly effort—logical, forceful, eloquent and convincing. His heart had been touched, his patriotism aroused, and all his intellectual faculties brought into full play. The *Congressional Globe*, in bold headlines, published it as follows:

SPEECH OF HON. RUSSELL SAGE,
Of New York
In the House of Representatives,
August 6th, 1856,
The House being in the Committee of the Whole on the State of the Union.

"When I took my seat here in December, 1853, I found a new Administration in power, having been elected by one of the largest popular votes ever given to any previous one. It had two-thirds of its friends in the Senate and in the House. It received this power by professions and pledges of adherence to the compromises of the past, and opposition to the agitation of the question of slavery in the future. The country was in an unprecedented state of prosperity. Our foreign and domestic affairs were of the most pacific character; but in less than two months this change commenced, and instead of peace and quiet reigning, as had been promised, the firebrand of slavery and sectionalism was introduced into the Senate of the United States by the Senator from Illinois [Stephen A. Douglass]; and the unfortunate, bitter and sectional results that have followed forms the subject which I propose to discuss during the time allowed to me this evening in the following order, namely: Its causes, its objects, its results, its influence and its remedy.

"First, its cause was owing to the departure of the professions and pledges made prior to and at the commencement of the present Administration. It is a historical fact that during the long and exciting session of the Congress of 1850, certain Senators and Representatives then in Congress got up a Congressional pledge for the purpose of forever stopping the agitation of the subject of slavery, and of saving the Union, and that the present Administration came into power on the professions and pledges of, adherence to and support of this Congressional pledge and the compromise measures of 1850. Mr. Chairman, in order that we may fully realize the fidelity of this Administration in its professions and pledges, I beg to read the memorable document, that the country may judge of the difference between professions and acts.

"'*Declaration and Pledge.*—The undersigned members of the Thirty-first Congress of the United States, believing that a renewal of the sectional controversy upon the subject of slavery would be both *dangerous to the Union and destructive to its objects,* and seeing no mode by which such controversies can be avoided, except by a strict adherence to the settlement thereof, effected by the compromise passed at the last session of Congress, do hereby declare that their intention to maintain the same sentiment inviolate, and to resist all attempts to repeal or alter the acts aforesaid unless by general consent of the friends of the measure, and remedy such evils, if any, as time and experience may develop. And for the purpose of making this resolution effective, they further declare that they will not support for the office of President or Vice-President, or of Senator or Representative in Congress, or any member of the State Legislature, any man, of whatever party, who is not known to be opposed to the disturbance of the settlement aforesaid, and to the renewal in any form, of agitation upon the subject of slavery hereafter:

"'Henry Clay, Howell Cobb, Robert Toombs, Alexander H. Stevens, C. S. Morehead, William C. Dawson, Robert L. Rose, Thomas J. Rusk, Jeremiah Clemens, James Cooper, Thomas G. Pratt, William M. Gwinn, Samuel A. Elliott, David Outlaw, C. H. Williams, J. Philps Phoenix, A. U. Schermerhorn, John R. Thurman, D. A. Bokee, George R. Andrews, W. P. Mauquin, Jeremiah Morton, R. J. Rowie, E. C. Cabell, Alexander Evans, H. S. Foote, James Brooks, William Duer, M. P. Gentry, H. W. Hilliard, L. S. Hammond, Edmund Debeverry, H. Marshall, Daniel Breck, James L. Johnson, J. B. Thompson, J. M. Anderson, John B. Kerr, J. P. Caldwell, Allen F. Owen.'

"In January, 1854, a bill was introduced into the United States Senate by the Senator from Illinois [Mr. Douglass], providing for the organization of the Territories of Kansas and Nebraska; but it did not provide for the repeal of the Missouri restoration, and consequently it was recommitted to the Committee on Territories, and the wishes of the South complied with, and an outrage perpetrated towards the North that will never be forgotten, if it should ever be forgiven; because it was conceived in political bad faith and repudiation, and consummated by political intrigue, corruption and partisan rewards. When this bill, establishing the territorial government of Kansas and Nebraska, was passed, it was enacted that they should, when admitted as States, be admitted with or without slavery, as their constituents should provide. But this was not enough for the slaveholding States; and, therefore, the Missouri Compromise, which forbids slavery forever north of 36° 30′ north latitude, that time-honored compact, that bill of repose for which the slave-holding States had received and secured forever their consideration; that bill, which was a Southern measure, passed by Southern votes, and claimed as a Southern victory, that bill which was forced by the South on the North—

"But, sir, the North—although wronged, as she felt herself to be, by its passage—respected it and acquiesced in it; but the South, with their few dough-faced allies of the North, repealed it after it had been sanctioned for over a period of thirty years, and this, too, be it remembered, without there being a single petition presented to Congress asking for it. . . . . . And then came the novel experiment of submitting the subject to the people who should come into the Territory. This was done to admit slavery into that Territory which that compromise forbade; and if the North submits to its introduction she will deserve to bear all the reproaches that the South heaps upon her. . . . . . Well, sir, this breach of faith in the repeal of the Missouri compact was effected by making another plight of faith; that is, by providing that the settlers of Kansas 'should be perfectly free to form and regulate their domestic institutions in their own way.'"

Mr. Sage, referring to the immigration from different States of the Union, said: "Has the Executive or the Congress kept their promise and executed that law? No, sir, it has not been done; the disclosures made by the report of the special committee sent to Kansas establish the fact that of the 6331 votes cast in March, 1855, for the election of the Legislative Assembly of Kansas, 4921 of them were cast by armed bands of the inhabitants of Missouri, who invaded Kansas for that purpose on that occasion; that only 1410 legal votes were cast, and the majority of those were for the free-State candidate, though most of the free-State voters were driven from the polls. . . . . The people in the Territory have not been left free, but have had their homes invaded and subjugated, and they are, and their institutions have been, controlled by the people of Missouri; the arms of that State have been used against the free-State immigrants going to Kansas, by the tyrannical laws passed by that Assembly, and more tyrannically enforced by the officers by them appointed. The President of the United States has aided to enforce these laws, passed by usurpation and fraud. The complaints and appeals of the people in said Territory have been made in vain; their representations have been treated with indifference and neglect; the property of the free-State people has been destroyed and stolen; their buildings have been burned; their printing offices have been suppressed to prevent their making known the oppression, crimes and atrocities under which they were subjected; the people have been hunted out; they have been hung; they have been murdered; their cattle killed in their presence; they have been warned, one after another, to leave the Territory, by violence, in large numbers. Yes, Mr. Chairman, you may find them fleeing from the midnight blaze of their own dwellings. You may find their bones bleaching on the green fields of their new country. You may find some of them here at the capitol of the nation, this very day, who have been indicted by this mockery of justice in Kansas for constructive treason, imploring the Executive and beseeching Congress to do something, so that they may be allowed to have a fair and impartial trial by a change of place of trial to St. Louis, or any other place, except in Kansas, where there is not the first principle of justice administered towards free-State men." Mr. Sage then quotes from the Senate report, which confirms all the statements he had made regarding the gross injustice and inhuman treatment of these people by the Kansas authorities, and then continues:

"Having thus spoken of the cause of the present crisis in domestic affairs, I proceed to consider the contemplated objects to be attained by the report of the 'Missouri Compromise Act,' which I believe to be the extension of human slavery into Kansas and Nebraska. . . . .

"Down to the period of the commencement of the first Congress under General Taylor's administration, when a small number of Representatives from the South, led by two Representatives from Georgia [Toombs and Stevens], defeated the re-election of Hon. Robert C. Winthrop as Speaker of the House, because he would not commit himself by a pledge on the subject of slavery, such as no honorable man could give—the principles of the Missouri restriction had been voted for or approved of by most of the eminent and leading men of the South. But from this period a new doctrine was proclaimed in behalf of the right of the slave power to extend slavery into any of the Territories of the United States, on the ground of its existence prior to the adoption of the Constitution; and, therefore, it is claimed that slavery is not dependent upon or subject to any of the provisions of the Constitution. Well, sir, this is a little ahead of any higher law that I know of. I believe we have power over the subject of slavery in the Territories. So thought, and so did the Congress in 1820, when the South passed the Missouri Compromise Act; when Charles Pinckney wrote a letter rejoicing over the result of its passage.

"This, Mr. Chairman, was Thomas Jefferson's view of the power of Congress over the subject of slavery in 1784, not only in the Territories, but in the States to be formed out of the Territories. So thought the Congress in 1787, when the ordinance of that date was adopted, excluding slavery from the Northwestern Territory. So thought the Congress of 1789, under the Constitution, which recognized and confirmed the ordinance of 1789, which was appointed by George Washington. So thought the Congress of 1800, which passed an act establishing a territorial government over the Territory of Indiana, which was approved by John Adams. So thought the Congress of 1805, in their act establishing a territorial government over Michigan. So thought the Congress of 1809, in their act establishing a territorial government over Illinois; both of which last named acts were approved by Thomas Jefferson. So thought the Congress of 1834, in extending the jurisdiction of Michigan over Wisconsin and Iowa, which was approved by Andrew Jackson. So thought the Congress of 1836 and 1838, in their acts, also, establishing territorial government over Wisconsin and Iowa, which were approved by Martin Van Buren. So thought the Congress of 1843, in their act establishing a territorial government over Oregon, which was approved by James K. Polk, Mr. Buchanan being a member of his Cabinet. So thought the Congress of 1853, in their act establishing a territorial government over the Territory of Washington, approved by Millard Fillmore. In all the aforementioned acts the slavery restriction or proviso of 1787 was incorporated, and slavery expressly prohibited. So thought Mr. Webster, in 1850, when he said that these compromises (1850) comprehend every inch of territory not disposed of by previous legislation."

Mr. Sage cited many other authorities, and quoted from a letter of Millard Fillmore, of October 17, 1838, in which he replied to every question put to him by the Anti-Slavery Society in the affirmation. He quoted also from Henry Clay, who said, in 1850: "I repeat that I never can, and never will vote, and *no earthly power* will make me vote, to spread slavery over territories where it does not exist."

After giving statistics, comparing the population of the free and slave States in the Union, Mr. Sage said:

"Thus it will be seen that the number of slave-owners, including men, women and children, is only about three hundred and forty-one thousand, and the free white population are six millions, in the slave States—or only about one in twenty of the white population in the slave States are slave-owners. Yet this small number, by a union of interest, and by the political importance given to slavery, rule these States absolutely and despotically; the great majority of the people—a majority of nearly thirty to one—are never heard of, and have no more power in those States politically than the slaves its aristocratic rulers own! This is truly astonishing! But the condition of the General Government is more so. The free population of the Union is about twenty millions. The slave-owners now number some three hundred and forty-six thousand. For the past sixty years this number would average from one hundred and fifty to two hundred thousand; yet the General Government is in their hands, and has been for the past fifty years, when the majority against them in the Union is as sixty to one; still they hold the power, and the Government is directed and controlled by them, and has been almost ever since it has been in operation. And during all that time more than one-half the important offices of the Government—and I believe nearly two-thirds of those offices—have been filled by slave-holders to the exclusion of the great mass of the people of the United States.

"The five purchased slaves States—Florida, Texas, Arkansas, Louisiana and Missouri contain 543,368 square miles. The territory thus added to the slave States by purchase, is larger by 89,025 square miles than the five States named. This excess is a a larger territory than is contained in seven of the free States, *and this was all purchased ot extend slavery;* while the free States admitted have been formed out of territory belonging to the United States when the government was established, and to which the ordinance of Jefferson and of freedom, prohibiting slavery, was applied by the fathers of the Republic.

"The fifteen free States have 13,000,000 of free, white inhabitants; the fifteen slave States have 6,000,000; yet each have thirty Senators. True, the small States are entitled to two Senators each, as well as the larger ones; but this number of slave States extended over a large territory with a small population, make the disproportioned representation of the two sections in the Senate palpably unjust. In Senators, the slave States have, by this system kept up a representation in the proportion of two to one as against free States.

"In the House, the slave States' ninety members representing 6,000,000 of population; the free States' one hundred and forty-two members, representing 13,000,000. Upon the same rate with the slave States the free States should have one hundred and ninety-five members, a loss of fifty-three in the popular branch of the Government; that in which the popular voice is to be heard and the popular will expressed"

Mr. Sage then takes up the condition of the several free States, comparing each of them with the slave States and says: "These eleven States (Virginia included) that gave in 1852 a less vote than New York for a president, have *twenty-two* Senators, while New York has only two.

"Slaveholders have political advantages denied to all other men! A man who owns one thousand slaves has the same political power over his slave property as six hundred inhabitants in the free States. His power is superior to that of most of the voters in a town of ordinary size. He has, besides, individually, the same political power as the richest man in a free State. This additional right—six hundred strong—is solely in consideration of his owning one thousand slaves as property."

Referring to the aquisition of territory by the slave States he continued: "Yet the free States have paid more than two-thirds of the entire cost of these acquisitions of territory, and the consequent expenditures since incurred. They have borne their full share in the wars which led to or resulted from these aquisitions, in the expenditure of money and in the sacrifice of human life."

Again reverting to the political affairs of Kansas and Nebraska he shows how these territories in their legislative enactments constantly disregard and violate the Constitution of the United States. In closing this part of his speech Mr. Sage says: "Time will not permit me to go further into these Kansas laws which Senator Clayton declared to be an outrage upon the rights of the people and the civilization of the age in which we live." Mr. Sage also quotes from the *Detroit Free Press,* which declared, "But the President should pause long before treating as treasonable insurrection the action of those inhabitants of Kansas who deny the binding authority of the Missouri Kansas Legislature; for, in our humble opinion, a people that would not be inclined to rebel against the acts of a legislative body forced upon them by fraud and violence, would be unworthy the name of American. If there was even justifiable cause for popular revolution against a usurping and obnoxious government that cause has existed in Kansas."

"But, sir," says Mr. Sage, "notwithstanding this appeal, the President of the United States has declared in his special message to Congress, in his proclamation, and in his orders to Gov. Shannon and Colonel Sumner, through the Secretary of State and Secretary of War, that this code of territorial laws shall be enforced by the full exercise of his power. He knows their provision. He knows that these laws are in violation of the organic law organizing the Territory which he signed. He knows they are in violation of the Constitution of the United States which he and we have sworn to support."

During the debate a member from Alabama arose and endeavored to show that the slaveholders of the South came from a superior race of people with an ancestral line of which they had reason to feel proud, evidently thought that this fact ought to receive due consideration. He said:

"Members from the North seem to think that the reason why the South has had so large a share in our governmental operations lies in the institution of slavery. I tell them they are mistaken; it lies behind that institution. It is to be found in the administrative faculty belonging to the early settlers of the State—the Cavaliers and Huguenots, and which their descendants have inherited." Mr. Sage replied:

"Well, sir, I rejoice in the boldness of this boast of superiority of birth and blood. I respect and honor the frank expression of one's sentiments as thus given; but I tell the gentleman that he is mistaken in the true character of the people of the North. True, they have not enjoyed the advantages of experience that the people of the South have in the governmental affairs of the Government, but this is solely owing to the sectional and aggressive spirit of the slave power. But, sir, the people of the North will not long remain under the vain and boasting charge; they intend to demand, and expect to receive, and take their fair and just proportion of the responsibilities in the administration of the Government.

"If the people of the North are true to themselves, true to the best interests of their country, true to the Constitution and Union, as I know them to be, they will take the affairs of this Government into their own hands on the 4th of March next; and then the gentleman from Alabama will have an opportunity of witnessing the honor, capacity, and justice of the people of the North to administer the affairs of the Government."

In closing, Mr. Sage gives the remedy for the settlement of the disturbed conditions of the country. He says: "The remedy for the present unhappy state of affairs existing between the different sections of the country, is in a return to the principles of the early fathers of the Republic in the admission of Kansas as a free State for which we have precedents in the admission of Michigan and California, for which we have the approval of Judge McLean, who said in his letter to Chief Justice Hornblower of New Jersey, on the 6th of June last: "I have no hesitation in saying that the immediate admission of Kansas as a State into the Union under the Constitution already formed, commends itself to me as a measure of sound policy, and well calculated to bring peace to the Territory and to the Country."

"Oh, sir, if the South will pass the bill sent to it, restoring the Missouri Comprise restriction which protects the Territory to freedom north of 30° 30′ north latitude forever, and liberates the freemen of Kansas that are unlawfully imprisoned there; and provide for the reorganization of the territory until it is admitted into the Union as a State, they will do an act of justice which the country demands. Are not these just, reasonable and easy remedies—the true ones to restore peace and transquility in Kansas, and throughout the country?"

This speech of Mr. Sage made a most profound impression on the people of the whole country, who were led to realize the gross injustice toward the people of Kansas and Nebraska. It did probably more to precipitate the great events that followed than any other public speech of that period.

Referring to the great public work accomplished in the State and National councils by Mr. Sage, the Brooklyn *Eagle* in its issue of July 23, 1906, said, editorially: "New York city was the scene, and the enterprises centering there were the subject of Mr. Sage's greatest industry, patience, shrewdness and concentration during his very long life. Troy, however, is where he began work of saving and investment. There he also disclosed those qualities, which made him conspicuous as a public man. In Troy also is situated the institution to which Mr. Sage is known to have contributed. There was the theatre of the discoveries of his abilities and of his effective use of them as a storekeeper and as a speculator. There, also, was the scene of his early identification with public affairs, as a supervisor, as a county treasurer, as a member of two national congresses, as one of the organizers of the Republican party, as one of the ablest of William H. Seward's friends, and as one of the advisers and upholders of Abraham Lincoln in the latter's first presidency. They reflected on and felt for Mr. Sage more honor than Manhattan ever did or felt for him.

"It is well to look at the Russell Sage of Troy. That man was a politician in the not bad sense of the word. He believed in the conservative Whiggism of Seward, and the support of the conservative Whig election of Zachary Taylor. He influenced that President to give to Seward's friends the Federal patronage which Seward's Whig opponents sought for themselves and for the undoing of Seward in politics. The Troy Sage afterward took part in the formation of the Republican party and in the endeavors to elect Fremont to the Presidency. He shared in the honorable failure to make Seward President in 1860, which resulted in the discovery of Abraham Lincoln. From that time the sequence of the reestablishment of the Union and the Emancipation of the slaves.

"All this involved settled purpose, a degree of moral courage, and a devotion to liberty. Identifications with these results made labor for them a valuable inspiration and instruction. With them for Mr. Sage was involved four years membership of the congresses which secured our territory to freedom, and which educationally prepared the North for Republicanism, and the Republicanism itself for the stewardship of the great purposes it long subserved and to which under Roosevelt, it is in part still committed in our history.

"As indivisible Union, opposition to the extension of slavery, the overthrow of rebellion, and the accomplishment of emancipation were the results which still stir the pulses, broaden the heart and glorify the brain. They outclass civil service reform, specie payments, expansion, the curbing of corporations and natiornal irrigation, the the creation or the enrichment of educational institutions and any other of the contemporary causes which broaden and better, and beautify our present life.

"None of these contemporary results would have been possible with slavery perpetuated, with Secession recognized, and with the breaking up of our Union into a series of petty republics, wrangling as well as petty. Mr. Sage's earlier life confronted and helped accomplish the greatest achievements of our nineteenth century politics. Had his career not extended beyond that limit, his fame had been more, his usefulness more, and only his wealth less.

"Those who think we exaggerate his political importance at that time should now recall that the second election to Congress was marked by the largest majority any human being ever won in his district, and was followed by his appointment on the Committee on Ways and Means. That is a distinction which not ten Congressmen in all our national history ever won, after so short a period of service. And his career in politics was advanced as well as interpreted by speeches which still survive as arguments for freedom and for union in our political annals."

On all occasions Mr. Sage jealously guarded the rights of the House against what he considered the infringements of the Senate. On March 3, 1857, after boldly criticising what appeared to him an act of gross injustice by the Senate, the Speaker ruled that "it was clearly out of order to refer to the proceedings of the Senate."

Mr. Sage replied that "there was something which took place in another place that would justify the members of this House, if they entertain that respect for themselves, which I think they do, in standing firm upon what they believe to be their rights. There was every concession made at the first conference to meet the views of the committee upon the report of the Senate; so much so that they signed a report. After that concession upon the part of the House the report was submitted to the Senate, but it was not received. On the contrary, there were threats thrown out that if the Senate only adhered, they would make the House do as they had made them do before. The result has been a second committee of conference.

"In addition to that resolution, which passed the House by almost unanimous consent yesterday, it has been treated in the same manner. No disposition has been manifested to comply with the wishes of the House, though expressed by a two-thirds vote. But I will not consume the time of the House in discussing this matter. I hope the House will stand firm, and let the Senate understand that we have some rights as well as the gentlemen at the other end of the Capitol."

Melatiah E. Dwight, in *The New York Genealogical and Biographical Record* for October, 1906, in referring to Mr. Sage's public career, said: "In 1848 he was a delegate to the National Convention of the Whig party. He controlled twenty-eight out of the thirty-two New York delegates, and took a leading part in the nomination of

General Zachary Taylor for the presidency. It was at his suggestion that the Convention nominated Millard Fillmore for Vice-President. This selection by Mr. Sage of Fillmore for Vice-President made him President, for General Taylor died while in office and Fillmore succeeded him. The part taken by him in General Taylor's nomination gave him much influence with the President, and when the latter disregarded the nominations for federal office made by Mr. Seward, who was then United States Senator for New York, Mr. Sage was chosen as the best representative of the Seward Whigs, to convince the President that his prejudices were unfounded. He visited Washington, saw General Taylor, and was entirely successful in his mission. In 1850 Mr. Sage was nominated for Congress by the Troy Whigs, but owing to the defection of a faction of the party opposed to Mr. Seward, he was defeated. He was again nominated in 1852, and was elected by a small majority. Two years later he was returned to Congress by the unprecedented majority of seven thousand votes. During his four years in Congress the great talents of Mr. Sage in financial matters found recognition in his appointment as a member of the Ways and Means Committee, the most important committee of the House. He served also on the Invalid's Pension Committee, which had charge of the pensions incurred by the Mexican War, and took part in the five weeks' struggle which finally resulted in the election of Nathaniel P. Banks as Speaker. But the incident in his Congressional career which brought him most reputation was the appointment of a committee through his efforts to inquire into the condition of Washington's old estate at Mount Vernon, Va. The committee's report bore fruit in the formation of the Mount Vernon Association, the purchase of the estate, and its dedication as a permanent memorial of the Father of his Country.

"At the end of his second term, notwithstanding his success in political life, Mr. Sage determined to abandon politics and devote himself exclusively to business. He, therefore, declined another nomination. The panic of 1857, which ruined so many, while it left him comparatively unscathed, had an important effect upon his business career. He had advanced considerable money in the La Crosse Railroad. To protect his loans he found himself compelled to advance yet larger amounts, and finally, through legal proceedings, to become owner of the road, which ultimately extended into the Chicago, Milwaukee and St. Paul system. This opened to him a wider entrance into the transportation business of the country. It would be hard to point to a man who took a greater part in the development of American railroads. During his career he achieved the presidency of no less than twenty corporations. He was connected in an official capacity, at one time or another, with the Iowa Central; Union

Pacific; Missouri Pacific; St. Louis, Iron Mountain and Southern; Wabash, Texas and Pacific; Troy and Bennington; Troy and Boston; Delaware, Lackawanna and Western; Chicago, Milwaukee and St. Paul; Manhattan Elevated, and other railroads. He was one of the largest stockholders in Manhattan Elevated, and took an active part in its management. One of his favorite ideas concerning elevated roads was that they should be double-decked, so that express trains might run on the upper tracks. Other enterprises in which he had been active are the Pacific Mail Steamship Company; the Mercantile Trust Company; the Importers and Traders National Bank; Western Union Telegraph; International Ocean Telegraph and American Telegraph and Cable Companies; the Standard Gas Light Company, and the Fifth Avenue Bank —of which he was one of the founders and the only one living at the time of his death.

"In 1863 Mr. Sage gave up his Troy business altogether, and removed to New York, to devote himself wholly to the promotion of his own and other railroads, and to operate in stocks. He opened an office in William Street, and gave his first attention to Chicago, Milwaukee and St. Paul securities. Later he extended his interest to other railroads, and gradually enlarged his field of operations until it covered nearly the whole range of stocks listed on the Exchange. He was unsurpassed as a judge of values, and his success became proverbial. It is said that only once did he sustain any great loss. This was at the time of the failure of Grant & Ward, in 1884. He was the originator of the system of the sale of privileges, and did a large business in what are known as 'puts' and 'calls.' He said that he started this business to assist brokers of moderate means. But it was as the largest operator in cash loans that Mr. Sage was generally known. Certainly no other individual did so large a business in lending cash on loans, subject to be called for payment at any time. With his millions lent under such circumstances, it is easy to perceive that in the event of his death, if all of his loans of this nature should be called in, serious disturbance in the price of securities might follow. It is illustrative of Mr. Sage's character that he took steps to avoid any such disaster. He prepared a special form of contract for all cash loans, whereby it was expressly stated that upon the death of the lender the loan should not be called merely for that reason. One of the features of Mr. Sage's financial career was his friendship with Jay Gould. They had come together as promoters of the Atlantic and Pacific Telegraph Company, which was later merged into the Western Union. Until Mr. Gould's death Mr. Sage counted the day lost in which he did not spend an hour with Mr. Gould at the luncheon prepared for the directors of the Western Union, of which Mr. Sage was one, until the time of his death. Their trust in each other was implicit. The fortune of either was ready to help the other out. Mr. Sage was the more astute of the two in the opinion of many.

"On December 4, 1891, Mr. Sage, while in his office at 71 Broadway, escaped instant death as by a miracle. An insane crank, Henry W. Norcross, of Somerville, Mass., entered the office, carrying a bag loaded with dynamite, and demanded that the sum of $1,200,000 be given him immediately or he would blow up the building. Mr. Sage saw that he was in the presence of a madman, rose and retreated from him, whereupon the maniac exclaimed, 'Well, then, here goes!' and lifting the bag high in air, dashed it violently upon the floor. The explosion which followed blew off the dynamiter's head, killed a clerk, injured others, and wrecked the office. Mr. Sage was much shaken, and received wounds in front, but was able to return to business in a few days. One of those most injured was William R. Laidlaw, who had called upon some brokerage business. Laidlaw brought suit for damages against Mr. Sage, claiming that the latter had seized him by the shoulder and swung him round, using his body as a shield against the force of the explosion. The jury awarded Laidlaw $25,000 damages. Mr. Sage was much criticised for refusing to pay this judgment. But he believed that he had not used Laidlaw as a shield, and naturally sought to defend himself against this imputation of his courage. He appealed from the verdict, and obtained a new trial, in which the jury failed to agree. At the third trial Joseph H. Choate appeared for the plaintiff, and obtained a judgment for $43,000. Again Mr. Sage appealed, and in January, 1899, the Court of Appeals reversed the judgment. 'There are certain physical facts,' so stated the Court in its opinion, 'established by the proof, and uncontradicted, which tend to show that the plaintiff's theory that he was in front of the defendant, was impossible. If, as claimed by the plaintiff, the defendant employed his body as a shield, and it was between him and the place of the explosion, it is quite difficult to comprehend how the missles which were found in the defendant's body in front and near the median line could have reached him.'

"No one can follow Mr. Sage's career without being convinced that he was a man of remarkable and varied powers. He could have succeeded in almost any field of action that he might have chosen. He could have continued in the political arena and become one of the foremost statesmen of this nation. He chose rather the largest, hardest and most dangerous field of all—the development of the transportation system of the country. For Mr. Sage, above all else, and from first to last, was a promoter and manager of railroads. That he was also a lender of money, particularly in his old age, was merely an incident in his long and useful life. 'He was an American, and loved his country,' said Henry Clews, on hearing of his death. 'He loved his country, believed in it, and was ready, therefore, to venture as well as labor in its behalf. He made it his purpose to assure and advance its prosperity.' 'My aim in life,' so he declared in an interview which was published Dec. 19, 1897, in the *New York Herald*, 'has been to do my share in developing the material resources of the country. I have spent millions on the railroad systems of the United States, and am now connected with more than twenty thousand miles of railroad, and with twenty-seven different corporations.'

"It has been said that Mr. Sage was 'a man of peculiarities.' If this means that he was a man of strong individuality it is measurably true. In several ways he was different from his associates. He loved work for its own sake, and found his greatest pleasure in doing it well. This was so marked a trait in his disposition that it was popularly believed he never took a vacation. While this was untrue, yet he himself has recorded his opposition to the vacation habit, saying that it was 'the outgrowth of abnormal business methods.' It is easy to say that he loved his work for its own sake, and say that he loved it rather for the gains it brought him. But greed is never just, although it is sometimes generous. Mr. Sage, however, was a just man. 'One of his peculiarities,' said John F. Dillon, in a warm tribute to him 'that stood out above all, was his integrity in everything, even to the smallest things.' Another of his traits was his frugality. It is this feature of his character which has provoked more criticism of Mr. Sage than any other. His name, indeed, has become a synonym for economy in the midst of riches. It may be questioned whether he did not render good service to his country by such a conspicuous example of simple living. But this is certain, it is of vastly more importance to the community that a man make his money honestly than spend it generously. The veriest miser who hoards his gold to gloat over it is immeasurably less of an enemy to society than the rich man who makes his millions by unjust methods, though he fare as sumptuously as Dives, and feed every Lazarus laid at his gate. Mr. Sage was honest and straightforward in all his dealings. It is true that he was surprisingly economical for one so rich, yet his frugality has been greatly exaggerated. He was unassuming in his disposition, and his personal wants were few. He cared little for luxuries, but those he wanted he enjoyed and paid for. He lived in a good house, and kept a good stable, for he loved horses, and his one pleasure, except business, was to drive them. He did not hoard his money, but caused it to circulate. Until far advanced in age, he staked it boldly in the promotion of the railroads and telegraphs of the country, and sometimes lost it—to all appearances with equanimity. He had, indeed, a horror of extravagance in any form; but this feeling is commendable. Another trait of his character was his fidelity. He was faithful to his word, his friends, his family, and to the many corporations in which he was a director. He stood firm and true for nearly half a century at the very center of trust in the financial world, and in the fierce and sometimes unfriendly light of publicity. He was an officer in twenty-seven great corporations, and for many years was in the thickest of the struggle for commercial advantages; yet never was his uprightness denied by his associates. As one of them has lately testified: 'His financial operations have always been without reproach.' He acknowledged, also, his religious and moral obligations. In his maturity, when thirty-four years old, he united with the Presbyterian Church of Troy, and since that time the churches of his choice have found in him a devout and constant worshipper. 'I have always tried,' he said, 'to do my duty to my brother man, and to the community in which I lived, and this will be a great comfort to me when I depart this life.'"

The *New York Times* said of Mr. Sage: "It would be hard to find a man who took a deeper interest in the development of American railroads than Mr. Sage. During his career he achieved the presidency of no less than twenty railroad corporations. He was, living, the only survivor of the original Board of Directors of the New York Central. He was connected in an official capacity, at one time or another, with the Iowa Central, Union Pacific, Missouri Pacific, St. Louis, Iron Mountain, and Southern Wabash, Texas and Pacific, Troy and Bennington, Delaware, Lackawanna and Western, Chicago, Milwaukee and St. Paul, the Manhattan, and other railroads."

Colonel Henry Watterson, the great democratic leader and editor of the Louisville *Courier Journal,* said of Mr. Sage:

"I knew Russell Sage from my early boyhood. When he first came to Congress from the Troy district, a very rugged pine knot, apparently from the backwoods; he lived at Willard's Hotel, where my father's family made their abode. I called him 'Uncle Russell' from the time I was twelve or thirteen years old until I last saw him ten or twelve years ago. During the Presidency of Dr. Green in the Western Union Telegraph Company—that is for twelve or fifteen years—I constantly met him at luncheon. He was always the same exuberant, affectionate, and apparently simple-minded man I had known in my childhood.

"The simplicity of Mr. Sage's life and the plainness of dress were proverbial, and his food was of the simplest and plainest kind, which may account in a measure for his great longevity."

Dr. Schmuck, his family physician, said of him: "After many years of close association with him, I can say that it was his home and his own family that he appeared at his best. He was considerate of every one who came near him, and tried to save them trouble and inconvenience."

Another, referring to the great helpfulness of his wife, said: "With her, Mr. Sage's home life was a happy one. Of all the good bargains he made, so his friends were wont to declare, his marriage to this estimable woman [Margaret Olivia (Slocum) Sage] was the best, and, among the maxims of Mr. Sage, to which he said that he owed his success, is one that intimates his own appreciation of her worth: 'The tender care of a good wife is the finest thing in the world.'"

Mr. Sage's first wife was Maria Winne, daughter of Moses L. Winne, of Troy, N. Y., to whom he was married in 1841; she died in 1867. Two years later he married Margaret Olivia Slocum, daughter of Hon. Joseph Slocum, of Syracuse, N. Y.

The Genealogical and Historical record of the Sage and Allied Families indicate the prevailing family traits which none can fail to recognize in the life of Russell Sage, notably his invincible courage, ardent patriotism, and unimpeachable integrity. Not one of his American ancestors, as the record proves, ever led a life of idleness, but by the "sweat of their brow they earned their bread." Industrious, self-reliant and independent they were, but with a due regard to the rights of others, and the happiness and comfort of their fellow-men. Part II. of this work contains the history of the Slocum and Allied Families—the line of Mrs. Margaret Olivia (Slocum) Sage, and includes many of the leading New York and New England families, notably, the Germains, Piersons, Josselyns, Browns, Standishes, etc.

Copy of Resolutions

and Expressions of Appreciation

of the Distinguished Services of

Hon. Russell Sage

by the Various Organizations of which

He was a Member

Deceased, July Twenty-second, 1906

Manhattan Railway Company

At a meeting of the Directors of the **Manhattan Railway Company**, held on Tuesday, the fourteenth day of August, Nineteen hundred and six, the following

Preamble and Resolution were offered by Mr. John Terry; and being seconded by Hon. Samuel Sloan were unanimously adopted

Whereas: At a ripe and extended age it has pleased Divine Providence to remove **Hon. Russell Sage**, who, since the ninth day of November, 1881, has been a Director and member of the Executive Committee of this Company; and who for twenty-five years has freely given to the service of this Company the benefit of his great experience in business affairs, his wisdom in solving the many difficult problems of the Company's existence, and his untiring industry in his attention to its interests;

Resolved: That this Board learns of his death with regret, and extends its sympathy to the members of his family at their loss.

His life illustrates the success that cannot fail to attend upon the untiring discharge of duty in connection with great pecuniary and business responsibilities.

His intelligence, his industry and thrift met with great and inevitable reward.

His public service while in Congress, while beneficial to his constituents, broadened his sphere of action and enlarged the field of his activities.

This Board desires to record its sense of his great service to this Company and its stockholders, and directs that this Resolution be entered upon its minutes, and a copy thereof be duly engrossed and sent to the widow of their departed colleague.

GEORGE J. GOULD,
President.

D. W. McWILLIAMS,
Secretary.

Texas and Pacific Railway Company

At a regular meeting of the Board of Directors of **The Texas and Pacific Railway Company**, held on Wednesday, September Nineteenth, Nineteen hundred and six, formal announcement of the death of **Mr. Russell Sage** having been made by the President, the following Resolutions in respect to his memory were adopted.

Resolved: That it is with deep regret that this Board recognizes the loss it has sustained in the death of **Mr. Russell Sage**, who, for twenty-six years served in its counsels, and brought to the performance of his duties the wise judgment, and integrity of purpose for which he was distinguished.

His eminent position in the world of finance, and intimate relations with corporate interests, rendered his counsels potential and of great value.

Resolved: That a copy of the foregoing Resolutions suitably engrossed be sent to the widow of Mr. Sage to whom the Board tenders its sincere sympathy in her bereavement.

George J. Gould	E. T. Jeffery
Samuel Sloan	Winslow S. Pierce
John L. Terry	J. J. Slocum
Howard J. Gould	A. S. Hopkins
John P. Munn	L. S. Thorne
Frank Jay Gould	T. T. Eckert
R. M. Gallaway	C. E. Satterlee

Wabash Railroad Company

At a special meeting of the Board of Directors of the **Wabash Railroad Company**, held Thursday, August Ninth, Nineteen hundred and six, the following Resolutions were unanimously adopted.

Voted: That this Board has heard with deep regret, of the death of **Mr. Russell Sage**, a Member of the Board since the organization of the Company, and one whose services were always at the command of the Company.

His good judgment always proved of benefit; and his associates desire to put upon record their appreciation of his many sterling qualities. He will be greatly missed by his associates, not only on this Board, but on others; and it is desired to record this expression of their regard.

Voted: That a copy of these resolutions be spread upon the minutes, and an engrossed copy sent to Mrs. Sage.

E. T. JEFFREY,
Chairman of Board.

Attest
J. C. OTTESON,
Secretary.

Iowa Central Railroad

The Directors of the Iowa Central Railway Company, of which Board Mr. Russell Sage was an honored member, desire to place upon record their appreciation of his services to the Company during the many years of his connection with it, and their personal tribute to his memory.

Mr. Sage became a Director of the Iowa Central Railway in February, 1889, and filled that position until the time of his death. He was Vice-President in September, 1889; and in the following year became President, which office he held until September, 1897; and, with the exception of two years, he was a member of the Executive Committee from 1889 to 1904. During the entire period of his connection with this Company, Mr. Sage gave to its interests the close attention, and served it with the fidelity so characteristic of the man; never failing of attendance upon the meetings of the Board except in case of illness; while, by his uniform courtesy and geniality, he won the esteem and sincere regard of all his associates.

Resolved: That this minute be spread upon the records of the Company and that a copy of the same, suitably engrossed, be sent to Mrs. Sage.

A. C. DOAN,
Secretary.

This was accompanied by the following letter.

Iowa Central Railway Co.
OFFICE OF PRESIDENT
Broad-Exchange, 25 Broad St.
EDWIN HAWLEY, President

New York, Sept. 14, 1906.

Mrs. Russell Sage,
Lawrence, L. I.

My Dear Mrs. Sage:

As a personal friend of your husband as well as on behalf of the Board of Directors of the Iowa Central Railway Company, I beg to tender you the accompanying Memorial in which we have attempted to express our sincere appreciation of his sterling qualities, and our profound regret, that in the evitable course of events he should be removed from amongst us.

Very truly yours,

E. HAWLEY.

Western Union Telegraph Company

Extract from the Minutes of the Executive Committee of the Board of Directors of the **Western Union Telegraph Company**; meeting held, July 25, 1906:

The Chair announced the death, since the last meeting of **Mr. Russell Sage**; whereupon the following was adopted:

In the death of Mr. Sage this Company has lost a loyal friend and one of its warmest supporters.

For twenty years he was a member of the Board of Directors, and of all the principal committees; and as long as his health permitted he was faithful in attendance upon the meetings, and took an active part in the direction of the Company's affairs.

Resolved: That the Committee gratefully records its appreciation of Mr. Sage's faithful service, and its acknowledgement of his sturdy independence of character and of the unassuming simplicity of his manner.

Resolved: That this Committee sympathize deeply with the family in their affliction, and that a copy of this Minute be sent to them.

A. R. BREWER,
Secretary.

New York Stock Exchange

The members of the New York Stock Exchange having been informed of the death of their former associate, Russell Sage, desire herewith to extend to the family of the deceased their sincere sympathy for the loss sustained.

H. K. LOWRY,
President.

New York, July 23, 1906.

Fifth Avenue Bank

At a meeting of the Board of Directors of the **Fifth Avenue Bank** of New York, held July 26th, 1906, the following Minute was adopted:

A large majority of the founders of the **Fifth Avenue Bank** have passed away. One of this number the **Hon. Russell Sage**, died on July 22, 1906.

Mr. Sage in his early manhood was a member of Congress, and a follower of the principals and policy of Henry Clay.

He was for many years a power in financial circles of New York.

His long and ceaseless activity included the period when the great railroads of the country were created, and the later era of the consolidation and reorganization.

He was a director in many important corporations, and left his impress upon the progress of this country for three generations.

Mr. Sage was for thirty years a prominent and useful member of the Board, and his strong and genial personality will be long remembered by his associates.

The foregoing was ordered to be spread upon the Minutes, and a copy be sent to Mrs. Sage with an expression of the cordial sympathy of the members of this Board.

A. S. FRISSELL,
President.

B. H. FANCHER,
Cashier.

The Importers and Traders National Bank of New York

New York, July 24, 1906.

Mrs. Russell Sage,

Lawrence, L. I., N. Y.

Dear Madam:

At a regular meeting of the Board of Directors of The Importers and Traders National Bank of New York held this day, the following:

Preamble and Resolutions were unanimously adopted, and a copy of them is herewith transmitted to you in accordance with the provisions thereof:

Whereas: The Board of Directors of this bank have heard with deep regret of the death of their Associate Director and Vice-President, Mr. Russell Sage, when full of years at the advanced age of ninety, who has been a director of this bank since 1864, and the President since 1868; and desire to record their appreciation of him, and his services to this bank; therefore:

Resolved: That in the death of Russell Sage, the directors of the bank have lost a personal friend whom they esteemed most highly for his marked abilities, and for his many sterling qualities, and the geniality always displayed in his long association with them; and that the bank has lost a director and officer who, through his long years' connection with it, was ever thoughtful of its interests, jealous of its credit, giving to it freely the benefit of his wise counsel and advise.

Resolved: That this Preamble and Resolution be spread upon the Minutes of the bank and that a copy of them be sent to his widow, with the assurance of the deep sympathy of the members of this Board for her in her affliction and sorrow.

Yours respectfully,

H. H. POWELL,

Cashier.

United States Guarantee Company

111 Broadway

New York, August 15, 1906.

At a meeting of the Board of Directors of the **United States Guarantee Company**, held this day, the following **Resolution** was unanimously adopted:

Resolved; That it is with deep regret that the Directors have to record the recent death of **Mr. Russell Sage**, one of the incorporaters and a Director of this Company since its organization in 1890; and the officers of the Company are directed to convey to the widow of the deceased an expression of the sincere sympathy of this Board, and of the appreciation of Mr. Sage's character; of his wise and conservative counsel, and of his efforts in promoting their Company's interests.

A true copy from the Minutes.

DANIEL TOMPKINS,
Secretary.

New York, August 15, 1906.

Mrs. Russell Sage,
Lawrence, L. I.

Dear Madam:

I beg to enclose a copy of **Resolution** adopted at the first meeting of the Company's Directors occurring since the decease of Mr. Sage, and to convey the assurance of my respect and sympathy.

Very truly yours,

E. RAWLINGS,
President.

The Consolidated Coal Company of St. Louis

At a meeting of the Board of Directors of the Consolidated Coal Company of St. Louis, held in New York on October third, Nineteen hundred and six, it was unanimously

Resolved: That in the death of **Mr. Russell Sage**, a member of this Board since the organization of the Company; his fellow Directors feel that they have lost one whose judgment and experience were always at the service of the Company; and they desire to express their appreciation of the services he rendered, and of the unfailing support that he gave to the Company. The Board desires to put on record the expression of their regard.

Resolved: That a copy of these Resolutions be spread upon the Minutes, and an engrossed copy sent to Mrs. Sage.

GUY PHILLIPS,
Asst. Secretary.

Emma Willard Alumnae Association

In the death of the Honorable Russell Sage, Emma Willard Alumnae Association of New York feel that they have lost one of their best and most valuable friends.

From the inception of this Association he has shown the deepest interest in its welfare and progress, and in all ways in his power he has aided us in our work; and his removal from these earthly scenes is a personal grief to each and all of us.

His gift of Russell Sage Hall was most generous and timely; as it helped to restore to its pristine glory a famous institution, and enabled it to keep its place as the pioneer in America of the higher education of women.

In recognizing the indebtedness of our Association to him we wish to pay tribute to the noble worth of the man, and his many kind acts, which gave the assurance that his aims were of the highest.

Those who knew him best are the first to acknowledge the virtues of his manhood, his sterling integrity, his Christian Character, and the warmth of his friendship.

But if we mourn our loss, how terrible must his passing away be to Our Beloved President, for so many years his companion and associate in the work of his life; sharing with him pleasures and pains, as well as charities, and the labor of helping others. She made for him an ideal home, where he was always sure to find effection, sweet counsel and peace.

To her in this sad hour we tender our deepest sympathy, and we pray that in the years to come heaven's choicest blessings may be hers.

Now the silver chord is loosed, and the golden bowl is broken, and the spirit has returned to God who gave it. But we know on the resurrection mooning there will be for them a glorlous reunion.

COMMITTEE

Mrs. John C. Havemeyer
Mrs. Allen C. Washington
Mrs. Mary Knox Robinson
Mrs. Charles A. Edwards
Mrs. Charles E. Patterson
Mrs. Randolph W. Townsend
Mrs. William S. Searles
Miss Marie Stevenson
Mrs. Lucius Wilson
Mrs. Titus E. Eddy

Troy Female Seminary

At a meeting of the Trustees of the **Troy Female Seminary, Emma Willard School,** announcement having been made of the decease, July 22, 1906, of **Hon. Russell Sage**, a member of this Board, Benefactor of this institution, it was

Resolved: That there be included in its permanent records the following Minute:

In the death of **Russell Sage**, the **Emma Willard School** loses one of its oldest trustees.

One who, by his prominence in the financial world and by the sturdy integrity of his character, as well as by his generous gifts, dignified the office which he held.

Russell Sage Hall, erected through the munificence of Mr. Sage, is a **Monument** that reveals the impulses of a sturdy and manly heart in hours when free from the cares and ambitions of business, it was left at liberty to dwell on cherished things that had touched and strengthened it in the more quiet paths of life.

The Building is more than anything else his expression of admiration for noble devoted womanhood. It commemorates the impression that womanly gentleness, purity, aspiration and wisdom, were able to work upon a nature involved in the most engrossing and intricate of affairs.

Inspired by two earnest women, one Mrs. Willard, long since deceased, who stimulated his early efforts by wise encouragement.

The other, still living, ever at his side, alert to seek and glad to find objects of ennobling love and care.

He built to one, and for the other, Russell Sage Hall. It stands as if at a gateway to his inner life an unconscious tribute to himself.

In this hour of affliction, the Board emphasises this record that discloses so fairly a nature that was not wont to seek publicity.

Resolved: That the above Minute be communicated by the Secretary to the family of the deceased, and published in the papers of this city.

WILLIAM F. GURLEY, *Pres.*
EDGAR K. BELTS, *Sec.*

Troy, N. Y., July 23, 1908.

Rensselaer Polytechnic Institute

At a meeting of the Trustees of the Rensselaer Polytechnic Institute of Troy, N. Y., held on August 2, 1906, the following resolution was unanimously adopted:

The Secretary of the Rensselaer Polytechnic Institute is directed to enter in the minutes this Expression of Appreciation of the life and services of Hon. Russell Sage lately deceased.

For ten years one of our Trustees.

Rising to a position of world-wide prominence in finance, renowned alike for great ability, industry and integrity, leading a life of Simplicity and Uprightness, whereby he attained to an age rarely reached by man.

It is fitting that his associates in this Board testify to their appreciation of his unusual gifts and steadfastness; essentials to the highest success.

His Useful Life in the upbuilding of great enterprises and the conduct of large financial affairs points to the emphasis to be placed on untiring energy, intelligence and integrity.

The Board of Trustees take this opportunity of expressing their sympathy for Mrs. Sage in her great bereavement.

Let a copy of this minute be published in the daily papers, and let an engrossed copy be sent to the widow of the deceased.

ELIAS P. MANN,
Vice-President.

JOHN SQUIRES,
Secretary.

The Rensselaer County Society

The Rensselaer County Society in the City of New York deeply mourns the loss by death of its Fourth Vice-President, the **Honorable Russell Sage.**

This is the first death in the Society since its recent organization.

We desire in offering our profound sympathy to his widow, for so many years his beloved and faithful companion, to place on record a testimonial to his sterling character.

The City of Troy was honored for many years by the residence of Russell Sage, and in selecting him as its representative in some of the most important stations in public life. He never failed to fully and satisfactorily meet any responsibility that was placed before him.

Fearless, Faithful, Honest and Honorable, the splendid record of his long life is left without a stain.

In this time of reckless extravagance and luxurious display we may well have a lesson from the quiet, simple and successful life of this self-made man, who, overcoming all adversities, and with no adventitious aid, rose from poverty to wealth and finally wielded an influence—especially in the financial world—that few have been able to command.

We mourn the death of our honored and respected associate.

New York City, July the Twenty-sixth,
One Thousand Nine Hundred and Six.

John A. Sleicher, *President.*
Walter J. McCoy
Benjamin D. Benson
Jeauvard Simmons
William R. Newely
Committee.

The International Committee of Young Men's Christian Association

3 West Twenty-ninth Street, New York City

Army and Navy Department

Silver Bay, Lake George,
Aug. 6. 1906.

Mrs. Russell Sage,
Fifth Avenue, New York

Dear Mrs. Sage:

At a gathering of the Army and Navy Secretaries in conference here the undersigned were appointed a committee to express to you our deep sympathy and regret in your recent bereavement.

May you continually feel the blessed ministry of Him who "was a man of sorrows and acquainted with grief."

Very sincerely,

J. S. TICHENOR
OTTO D. HEISSENBUTTE

The University of Wooster

PRESIDENT'S OFFICE

Wooster, Ohio, July 31, 1906.

Mrs. Russell Sage,
New York.

My dear friend Mrs. Sage:-

I wish to express to you the sincere sympathy of the Board of Trustees, faculty and students of The University of Wooster, in the great loss which has come to you in the death of your beloved husband, Mr. Sage.

The partings of life are great sorrows. They come to us all. Sorrows seem to be the common lot of all mankind, and yet we, who have our faith in Jesus Christ sorrow not as those who have no faith, for we know that our dear ones are safe in the arms of Jesus, and that we, too, shall meet them with the redeemed around the Great White Throne.

I rejoice to see the testimony which Mr. Sage has borne concerning his beloved wife to all the world in his magnificent will. What an honor this first and foremost business man has conferred upon you to intrust to your wise heart and mind, the distribution of so vast a fortune. In so doing, he has endeared his name to every true husband and faithful wife. He has honored a married relation by keeping its vow to the letter unto the end of life.

May the God of peace and comfort come into your soul and make your remaining years most happy and most blessed, is our sincere wish and prayer.

Very sincerely yours,

LOUIS EDWARD HOLDEN,
President.

"Little Mother's" Aid Association

August 14, 1906.

My Dear Mrs. Sage:-

The Managers of the "Little Mother's" Aid Association at their last regular meeting passed resolutions expressing sympathy with you in the great loss you have sustained in the death of your husband, and desire to convey to you their deep felt condolence and warm appreciation of your sad bereavement.

Yours Sincerely,

EMILIE VAN BEIL,
Secretary.

THE SAGE AND ALLIED FAMILIES OF AMERICA

THERE has been much speculation and many conjectures regarding the origin of the Sage family, but the evidence to sustain the many theories advanced is lacking. The most sensible theory is that contained in the Patronimica Britanica, which states that it is "Probably a translation of Le Sage, still a very common French surname. It has reference to the wisdom and prudence of the original bearer; *Wise*, as an English surname is a precise analogue."

The same word may have been applied by different nationalities to indicate the character and reputation of an individual before the use of surnames, and, finally, like many others, adopted by some one family and continued by his descendants. But there is no evidence to show that any *one* of this name was the founder of the Sage family, or that there is any connection between these various families. The most probable conclusion is, that a family of this name came over with the Conqueror, and was the founder of the Sage family of England; and from this no doubt originated all the Sage families of New England. Wherever found, they appear to have been men of great will power, as well as men of culture and refinement. Though not numerous, the family, from a very early period, has been one of high social standing in England, and the armorial bearings show that members of it were honored with the degree of Knighthood by their sovereign for distinguished service rendered. The fleurs-de-lis in the arms indicate the French origin of the name; and the motto, "Not for himself, but for his country," seems to apply to every member of the family from the earliest period in its history down to the present time. The description given by Burke is—

Sage.

Arms—Per pale erminois and vert three fleurs-de-lis counterchanged.

Crest—A stag's head erased and erect proper.

Motto—Non sibi sed patriae (Not for himself, but for his country.)

So far as shown by the records in the Old as well as the New World, this motto has been characteristic of the family, and they have proved themselves to be "without fear and without reproach."

The stag's head in the crest indicates alertness, watchfulness, quickness of thought and action—conspicuous traits in the Sage character.

It is noteworthy that three of the greatest financiers and capitalists of the past century—Russell Sage, Jay Gould, and Cyrus W. Field—were all descendants of the founders of the Connecticut Colony—a Colony and State that has furnished some of the greatest jurists, statesmen, patriots, inventors, and learned men in every profession, the world has ever known.

A record in detail of "The Sages in the Revolution" is given in the History of Middlesex County, Conn., compiled under the supervision of Mr. Henry Whittemore, in which it appears that nearly every member of this family, of fighting age and physically qualified, was enrolled in the patriot army during the War of the Revolution; and the records of the War Department at Washington furnish additional evidence of this fact.

MILITARY RECORD IN THE REVOLUTION OF THE SAGES OF CONNECTICUT

It has often been said of the State of Connecticut concerning her supply of troops in the Revolution that she "robbed the cradle and the grave." It is doubtful if any village in New England of the same population as Cromwell, then known as Upper Middletown, furnished more, if as many, men in proportion than did this little village. Says the local historian: "They were in the earliest struggles at Ticonderoga, at Bunker Hill, at Boston, and with General Arnold in his disastrous Quebec campaign. Of this little band of patriots not a family of its size in Connecticut sent as many men into the field as did the Sage family. First on the list is that of Colonel, afterwards General, Comfort Sage. He entered the army as Lieut.-Colonel of Wadsworth's regiment, which went to Boston in March, 1776, took part in the battle of Bunker Hill and the several engagements in and around Boston, till the close of that campaign and the departure of the British from Boston.

When General James Wadsworth's Brigade was organized in the summer of 1776, Colonel Comfort Sage commanded the Third Regiment, and was engaged at the battle of Long Island, the retreat from New York to Harlem Heights, took part in the battle of White Plains, etc. In the latter engagement Colonel Sage had the full command of eight companies of General Wadsworth's Brigade, whose term of service expired December 25, 1776. He was soon after placed in command of the Twenty-third Regiment of State Militia, made up mostly of companies from Middletown and Chatham.

When Tryon made his famous raid against Danbury, Conn., April 25-28, 1777, troops were hurried from every part of the State, and among the first to respond was Colonel Comfort Sage, who at this time was an experienced veteran.

General Comfort Sage was the son of Ebenezer, and grandson of John Sage. For some years after the close of the war he served as General of the State Militia, and added new lustre to the name of Sage.

"Nathan Sage, son of Amos, baptized August 23d, 1752; renewed baptismal covenant November 21st, 1773. In the privateering service, then the United States Navy. While the British were blockading New York, Sage, as Captain on a vessel, ran a cargo of powder into port, after a sharp race with two British cruisers. Was received by Congress, then in session in New York. After the war Captain Sage was appointed Collector of the Port of Oswego, N. Y., which position he held till his death, about 1833, being then eighty-four years old.

"Elisha Sage, another son of Amos, was a private in the war.

"William Sage, another son of Amos, born 1749, was a captain, and was engaged in the battle of Bunker Hill.

"Epaphras Sage, born 1757, was a private in the war, and was afterwards Ensign, Lieutenant, and Captain of Militia; he died May 28, 1834, aged seventy-seven.

"Matthew Sage, killed in battle, in 1776; probably at the battle of Long Island, in which his cousin, Colonel Comfort Sage, bore a conspicuous part.

"Benjamin Sage was with Arnold in the Quebec campaign.

"Simeon Sage, son of Deacon Solomon Sage, three years in the service.

"David Sage, jr., died from wounds received at Quebec, 1776.

"Daniel Sage, with Arnold in Quebec campaign.

"Hosea Sage, died in service in 1781, at West Point."

It is doubtful if another family in the whole State can show such a record as this.

The old cemetery at Cromwell, where the ancestors of Russell Sage resided, tells the simple story of the family, and of the esteem in which they were held by the community.

"Here lies interred the body of John Sage, who departed this life January 22d, A.D. 1751, in the 83d year of his life.

"He left a virtuous and sorrowful widow, with whom he lived 57 years, and had fifteen children, twelve of whom married, and increased ye family by repeated marriages, to the number of twenty-nine, of whom there are fifteen alive. He had one hundred and twenty grandchildren, one hundred and five of them now living; forty great grandchildren, thirty-seven of them now living; which makes the numerous offspring one hundred and eight-nine."

This is upon a slate tablet set in a freestone table monument. Upon a second tablet of slate, in the same stone, is the following inscription:

"Here lies the body of Mrs. Hannah Sage, once the virtuous consort of Mr. John Sage, who are both covered with this stone, and these has been added to the numerous offspring mentioned above; forty-four by births and marriages, which makes the whole two hundred and thirty-three. She fell asleep September the 28th, 1783, in the 85th year of her age."

"Sacred to the memory of Amos Sage, who died at Port-au-Prince, January 25, 1791, in the 18th year of his age. Much lamented by his father, mother, sister and friends, he bid fair to make the honest man."

Remarkable as it may appear, it was stated in 1883 that "none of the descendants of John Sage and his numerous offspring reside in town. Also, that there are five hundred and five families descended from him scattered through thirty-four States and territories."

It will be noticed that the Sage family was remarkable for the longevity of its members when they died from natural causes. They were a vigorous, hardy race, noted for their courage and endurance.

David Sage, the first of the name in New England, was born in 1639, and came with his mother, a widow, to Middletown (then known by the Indian name of Mattabesett), in 1652, one year after it was "ordered and decreed that Mattabeseck shall be a Towne." Rev. David Dudley Field, who published a small history of Middlesex County, Conn., in 1819, states that he came from Wales; but there is not a particle of evidence in the records to support that statement. If they came from Wales, their parents must have gone there from England, as the name is not found in the records of the Welsh families.

The Town Records of Middletown show that on "Feb. 22, 1662, David Sage was admitted an inhabitant of Middletown." If the date of his birth is correctly given, he was at that time twenty-three years of age, and his first marriage occurred two years later. In Vol. II., Connecticut Colony Records, is the following:

"At a Court of Election, held at Hartford, May 9, 1667, a list of those Nominated to Election for Deputies." Then follows another list: "These were sworne." Of the list of "sworne," containing twenty-eight names, the name of David Sage appears among them. He was a man of great industry and preservance, and one of the most thrifty farmers in the town. His "home lot" and residence was at Middletown "Upper Houses," now known as Cromwell. He died there March 31, 1703. He left a large estate for those days. He raised a large family of children; and after making liberal provision for all those living at the time of his death, he says: "The rest of my estate, personal and real, I leave with my wife, to be managed by my sons Jonathan and Timothy, so that she have a comfortable and creditable maintenance during her natural life, and at her decease to be shared betwixt sd Jonathan and Timothy—debts and legacies paid."

Mr. Sage married, first, in Feb., 1664, Elizabeth, daughter of John Kirby; she was born Sept. 8, 1646; she "deceased about the 23d year of her life," leaving three children, viz.:

Daniel, born Feb. 1, 1665.

Elizabeth, born Jan. 1, 1666.

John, born March 6, 1668.

David Sage married, secondly, Mary Wilcox, daughter of John Wilcox, one of the original settlers of Hartford, Conn. He and his brother Thomas were early settlers at Middletown "Upper Houses," now Cromwell. By his second wife, Mary Wilcox, David Sage had issue:

Mary, born Nov. 15, 1672; married to Dr William Johnson, the first President of Kings (now Columbia) College, New York.

Jonathan, born 1674.

Timothy Sage, born Aug. 14, 1678 (see record).

Nathaniel, born 1680; died without issue.

Mercy, born 1680, twin of Nathaniel.

Timothy Sage, second child of David, by his second wife, Mary Wilcox, was born in Middletown, Conn., Aug. 24, 1673. He married Margaret Hulbert, daughter of John, son of Thomas Hulbert, the ancestor first of Saybrook, then of Wethersfield. Lieut. Thomas Hulbert came to this country in the barque Bachelar, in 1635, with Lion Gardner, to build a fort at Saybrook, at the mouth of the Connecticut river. The Pequots made an attack on Gardner and his party while absent form the fort, and Hulbert, though severly wounded, fought his way back to the fort inch by inch. Gardner, in his account of the affair, says: "But in our retreat I kept Thomas Hulbert, Robert Chapman and John Spencer still before us, we defending ourselves with our naked swords, or else they had taken us all alive." Thomas Hulbert also took part in the assault on the Pequot fort, on the Thames River, under Mason, which resulted in almost the entire extinction of the tribe. He afterwards settled in Wertersfield, Conn.

In the Connecticut Colony Record, Vol. VII., is the following, as a part of the record of the General Court:

"Upon the petition of Margaret Sage, of Middletown, administratrix on the estate of Timothy Sage, late of Middletown, deceased, prays to this Assembly that she, with the assistance of Captain William Savage, of said Middletown, may be empowered to sell so much of the lands of the said Timothy Sage, deceased, to the value of £39 6s. 4d., by and with the advise of the Court of Probate, Hartford."

Timothy Sage, by his wife, Margaret (Hulbert) Sage, had issue:

Samuel, born 1709.
Timothy, born 1714.
David, born 1718.
Solomon, born 1729.
Amos Sage, born 1724 (see record below).
Two daughters, Mercy, born 1712; Mary, born 1716.

Amos Sage, youngest son of Timothy and Margaret (Hulbert) Sage, was born at Middletown Upper Houses (now Cromwell, Conn.), 1722. He married Rebecca Wilcox, of Cromwell, daughter of Francis, son of Samuel, Son of John Wilcox, the ancestor. "The Wilcox family," says a well known authority, "is of Saxon origin, and was seated at Bury St. Edmunds, in County Suffolk, England, before the Norman Conquest." Sir John Dugdale, in the Visitations of County Suffolk, mentions fifteen generations of this family prior to 1690. This takes the family back to 1200. In the reign of King Edward III. Sir John Wilcox was entrusted with several important commands against the French, and had command of the cross-bow men from Norfolk, Suffolk and Essex. On the ancient records the name is spelt Wilcox, Wilcocks, and Wilcockson (meaning the son of Wilcox). The coat armour of this family is described as—

Arms—Argent a lion rampant between three crescents sable; a chief vair.

Crest—Out of a mural coronet, or, a demi lion rampant, sable, collared vair.

Amos Sage, by his wife, Rebecca (Willcox) Sage, had issue:

Amos, born 1747.
William, born 1748.
Hezekiah, born 1750.
Nathan, born 1752.

Elisha Sage, born 1755 (see record below).
Rebecca (Riley), born 1754.
Abigail, born 1758; married —— Swift.
Submit, born 1759; married —— Willetts.

Elisha Sage, fifth child of Amos and Rebecca (Willcox) Sage, was born 1755. He served as a private in the War of the Revolution. He was an industrious, enterprising farmer and public-spirited citizen. He married Martha Montague, daughter of John Montague, son of Richard, son of John, son of Richard, the American ancestor. He was the son of Peter and Eleanor (Allen) Montague, son of William and Margaret (Malthouse), son of Robert and Margaret (Cotton), son of William Montague, of Buckinghamshire, England.

The Montague family have borne an important part in the history of England from the time of the Conqueror down to the eighteenth century. In the old Chronicles of France mention is made of forty-seven different incursions by various Scandinavian bands called Northmen. The most important of these, under the command of Rollo, the Dane, resulted in the permanent occupation of a large province, which was subsequently Normandy. "It was thus," says Freeman, "the settlement of these northern pirates which finally made Gaul French in the modern sense. It was at the same time the alliance with Romaine France which brought the Northmen fully under the influence of French language, law and custom which made them Normans, the foremost Apostles alike of French chivalry and Latin Christianity."

In this province and of this people, was born on the 14th of October, 1024, William, Duke of Normandy, known as William the Conqueror.

In this province also flourished one thousand years ago the Norman family of Montague. They were seated probably at Montagu les Bois, in the district of Constances, of which place it was said: "Its ancient lords were famous in the middle ages." The name and family of Montagu was probably well known and distinguished at that time as evidenced by the fact that there are mountains, castles, fortresses and towns, bearing this name.

Drogo de Montagu (or, as the Latin records give it, Montacute and Montacuté,) was born about 1040. He became the trusted companion, follower and intimate friend of Robert, Earl of Moriton, the favorite brother of William, Duke of Normandy.

Drogo and the Earl of Moriton were of the same age, and both of them entered heartily into the plans of William in his proposed expedition against England. Drogo de Monte-acuto accompanied the expedition in the immediate retinue of Robert, Earl of Moriton. They landed at Pevnesey, upon the coast of Sussex, late in September,

1066, and immediately burned and scuttled their ships that their only hope might be in their courage and resolution, the only safety in victory.

This marked the advent of the first Montagu upon the shores of England, and, as he marched toward the plain near Hastings, where the battle was fought he bore the kite shaped shield of the Norman invader, which contained a blue ground (azure), and the full length figure of a griffin segreant; (rampant, with wings expanded) this figure was of gold. This device was adopted later as the Montagu Coast of Arms.

[A gryphon or griffin was an imaginary creature devised by the ancients, and consisted of the body and tail of a lion with the head and talons of an eagle—thus denoting great strength and courage, united with great swiftness.]

Lady Cleveland in her description of the Battle Abbey and its associations, says: "But the principal features of the country are, of course, unchangeable. It was over yonder high hill to the left, crossed by the present road to Hastings, that the Conqueror came. There he vowed to build his Abbey, and formed his army in three divisions that were to make the attack; whence, it is said, is derived the name of Telham Hill. The right wing, commanded by Roger de Montgomerie, afterwards Earl of Shrewsbury, Chichester, and Arundel, and the founder of a great English house, was composed chiefly of soldiers from Picardy, Boulogne, and Poix, and charged up the steepest part of the hill where the houses of the Lower Lake now stand, and the road leads down to the station."

Joselyn de Bec of the old Normandy family of Josselyn, or Jossiline, who accompanied the expedition, was in all probality closely related to this Roger de Montgomerie and served with him or under him. A history of Normandy, published in 1767, contains a description of the Monastery of St. Martin at Troan, a small town an the Orne, says:

"A Benedictine Monastery, dedicated to St. Martin, the Bishop, founded in the year 1050 by Roger de Montgomery, *cousin to William the Conqueror* and Earl of Arundel, Chichester, and Shrewsbury. He was the son of Hugh de Montgomery and *Joscelus* his wife, daughter of Trerolph, lord of Pont Audimer, by Werd, sister to Gannord, wife of Richard II, Duke of Normandy. [This Joselyn de Bec—signifying of Bec—was the ancestor of Mrs. Russell Sage.]

It was the custom in those days for great military leaders to erect monasteries to some saint in the hope that intercessory prayers might be made for their own souls. The history of Normandy, previously referred to, states that:

"The edifices in Caen, which principally attract the attention of a traveller, are the two great Benedictine Abbies of St. Stephen and the Holy Trinity—the former for men and the latter for women. Historians agree that the Abbey of St. Stephen was built by William the Conqueror, and that of the Holy Trinity, by his Queen Maud or Matilda in pursuance of a mandate of Pope Nicholas II. in 1064. On the 13th of September, 1077, this church was, with great solemnity, dedicated to St. Stephen by John, Archbishop of Rouen.

"In the middle of the choir, and just before the high altar was deposited the body of its founder:—William the Conqueror, King of England, and Duke of Normandy, under a most stately monument, erected at the expense of his son, William Rufus, and richly adorned with gold, silver and precious stones.

"Within the precincts of this Abbey, and adjoining to the church, King William the Conqueror built a stately palace for his own residence.

"Upon the outside of the wall of the chapel were painted in fresco four portraits as big as life representing William the Conqueror, his wife Matilda, and their sons Robert and William. The Conqueror was drawn as a very tall man, clothed in royal robe, and standing on the back of an hound couchant.

"Queen Matilda was dressed in Kerthe and mantle, and had on her head a diadem; her feet were supported by the figure of a lion.

"Duke Robert was represented as standing on a hound. Upon his right hand clothed with a glove stood a hawk.

"The picture of Duke William represented him as a youth bareheaded, dressed. He also was represented with the left hand clothed with a glove holding a falcon, which he was feeding with his right."

"In the Abbey of the Holy Trinity at Caen is *A Tomb of the Foundress, Queen Matilda, Wife of William the Conqueror.* Queen Matilda, or Maud, was the daughter of Baldwin, surnamed the Gentle, Earl of Flanders by Adala or Alice, the eldest daughter of Robert, King of France, son of Hugh Capet. Duke William married her at Augi, in Normandy, while he was young. Upon his victory over Harold, being offered the crown of England, he would have deferred his coronation till Matilda came over to partake of the ceremony; but being pressed not to delay it, he was crowned by himself, and she afterwards, on Whit Sunday, in the year 1068.

While William was anxiously awaiting the arrival of his Queen to participate in this important ceremony an interesting scene transpired in Normandy. The author of the history of Normandy after discribing the suburbs of St. Sever, on the banks of the Seine, says:

"In the fields behind this magazine is the Benedictine priory of Notre Dame du Pre, or, as it is more generally called Bonnes Nouvelles founded in the year 1060 upon a spot of ground belonging to the *Abbey of Bec*, by Maud, wife of King William the Conqueror, at the fellicitations of Anselme, who afterwards became Archbishop of Canterbury. This priory was originally dedicated to the mystery of the Annunciation of the Holy Virgin, but, as the tradition of the place assures us, the Queen being at her devotions in the priory chapel, when she received the news of the complete victory gained by her husband over King Harold at Hastings, she, in order to perpetuate the memory of that important action, ordered that thenceforth the priory should be called Bonnes Nouvelles, (Good News). After the Conqueror's death, his eldest son, Robert, endowed this priory with the tithe of his part near Rouen, and annexed it to the Abbey of Beck, reserving to himself the power of erecting it into an Abbey, and making it again independent in case he should thereafter think fit. Maud, the daughter of King Henry I., had so great an affection for this priory that she became a considerable benefactor to it, and in 1135, portions of the body of King Henry I. were deposited under a handsome monument before the high altar in the ancient church of this priory. Maud, the daughter, was interred in the *Abbey of Bec.*"

William Montacute erected a Monastery at Montacute Mountain, and endowed it with the borough and Market of Montacute. The line was continued through Richard, his son, to Drue de Montacute, father of William de Montacute, who had son William, father of William (2), who had Sir Simon de Montacute; the latter was father of William, Lord of Montacute, whose eldest surviving son William, was made a baronet in the reign of Edward III. He was appointed Governor of Sherbourne Castle in the county of Dorsit, and in 1337 was constituted Admiral of the King's fleet, and the following year, in consideration of his faithful services in the Scottish wars, he was advanced to the title of Earl Salisbury. He married Catharine, daughter of Lord Grandeson, a famous Baron. She was a brave woman, worthy of such a brave and noble man as was her husband. She nobly defended and aided, with heroic valor, the defense of the castle of Werk, with her husband's brother, Sir Edward Montacute, who was its Governor; and she also defended bravely, her own Castle of Salesbury, from King David of Scotland, with the aid of William Montacute, her husband's cousin, while her husband was a prisoner in France.

Sir John Montacute, son of the former, was the third Earl of Salisbury, and his son Thomas was the Fourth.

The line of William Montacute or William Montague is continued in a direct line as follows:

William Montague, who erected a Monastery at Montacute. He had a son

Duke de Montacute, who was father of

William de Montacute in the sixth reign of Richard I. (1196), succeeded to the barony. His son William Montacute recovered all the lands his father had lost. He was Sheriff of Dorsetshire, Somersetshire, in the 6th, 7th, 8th and 9th reign of John (1205-1209). His son

William de Montacute, who had summons to attend the King into Gascony against Alphanso 10th, King of Castile, who had usurped the province. In the 41st reign of Henry III. he was summoned to be with the King of Chester on the feast day of St. Peter, *ad vincula,* well furnished with horse and armour, there to march against Llewellyn of Griffith, Prince of Wales. He had issue, by Bertha, his wife

Sir Simon de Montagu, who as Burke declares, was one of the most eminent persons of the period in which he lived. In the 14th reign of Edward I. he was in the expedition made into Wales, and within a few years after received considerable grants from the Crown. In the 22nd reign he was in the wars of France, where he appears to have been engaged for the two or three following years, and then we find him fighting in Scotland. In the 27th reign he was constituted Governor of Corfe Castle and summoned to Parliament as a Baron from 28th Edward I. to 9th Edward II. In the 4th Edward II. his lordship was appointed Admiral of the King's fleet then employed against the Scots, and he obtained in three years afterward license to make a castle of his mansion house at Perlynton in Somersetshire. He married Aufrick, daughter of Fergus, and sister and heir of Ovry, King of the Isle of Man, and had issue

William, his successor, and Simon

Baron William de Montacute, who was summoned to Parliament, was born 22nd August, 1318. This nobleman has distinguished himself in the Scottish wars in the lifetime of his father and was made a Knight of the Bath. In the 11th reign of Edward II., being then steward of the King's household, his lordship was constituted seneschal of the Duchy of Aquitaine, and had license to make a castle of his house at Kersyngton in Oxfordshire. He subsequently obtained other extensive grants from the Crown. He married Elizabeth, daughter of Sir Peter de Montford of Bearedesert, by whom he had surviving issue: William, his successor; Simon, Sir Edward, Katharine, Alice, Mary, Elizabeth, Hawise, Maud, Isabel. His lordship died in Gascony, in 1319, but was buried at St. Frides, now Christ Church Oxford.

It is a matter of considerable interest to the Montagu family that a decendant of Drogo de Montacute, who fought so valiantly under the Conqueror, finally came into possession of the Battle Abbey.

The Abbey had existed close upon five hundred years when it met its doom, on May 27, 1538, and passed, with all its possessions into the hands of Henry VIII's commissioners. The dissolution of the smaller monasteries, two years before, had warned the monks of the impending spoilation, and they had warily disposed of all their valuables. "So beggarly a house I never se" wrote Dr. Layton (one of the authors of the *Black Book*), "nor so filthy stuffe . . . . . . the vestments so baysse, worn and ragged, and torne as your lordshippe would not thinke." The monks were all pensioned; of sixty (their original number) sixteen only then remained. According to the usual practice, the chapter-house dormitory, sacristy, and cloisters were razed to the ground, and all the other buildings unroofed and dismantled. The great minster, with its campanile was pulled down "for lucre of the leade, tymber, etc.;" and the beautiful "Basilica," that had been so long in building was so rapidly and utterly demolished that the new owner planted his garden on its site."

This was Sir Anthony Browne, Master of the Horse, who, three months after the surrender, received a grant of the Battle Abbey and all its lands in Sussex and Kent, with the sole exception of one manor, reserved for the Chief Commissioner, Sir John Gage. This Sir Anthony was a high lineage, representing a branch of the old Norman house, of La Ferté, and the son of one of four great Montague heiresses, Lucy, Countess of Southampton, an able and sagacious man, who had spent all his life at Court, and as "the well-guided ship that could go with the tide," always remained in high favor. The King appointed him one of the executors of his will, and guardian of his younger children, the Princess Elizabeth being placed under his special care. It was intended that she should take up her abode at Battle Abbey, and he began to build a wing to the Abbot's house for her reception: but he did not live to complete it, and she never came. His effigy, with that of his first wife, remains on the altar tomb in Battle Church, that he is supposed to have erected himself.

Sir Anthony's son was created Viscount Montagu by Queen Mary, and built himself a stately mansion on what is believed to have been the site of the former Guest-house of the Monastery. But his chief residence was at Cowdray, where he entertained Queen Elizabeth right royally for a week, in 1501; and his successors lived there almost entirely. Battle Abbey was occasionally used as a dower-house, but as time went, it was more and more neglected and abandoned, and latterly became, in its deserted condition, the haunt of smugglers who stored their goods in the vaults. The third Viscount, who had suffered heavily in the Civil War, disparked the "Great Park," and his son sold the place to Sir Thomas Webster.

The next Lord Montagu, who married a Methodist of Lady Huntington's school, was the first of the family who left the Church of Rome. This yonng man and his friend, Mr. Sedley Burdett, while on a boating excursion on the Rhine, made a fool-

Battle Abbey as it was under the ownership of the Montagues

Battle Abbey as it is

hardy attempt to shoot the falls of Laufenberg. The authorities knowing the risk, did their best to prevent it, but in vain; they heeded neither warning, remonstrance, nor prohibition. Even at the last moment, Lord Montagu's servant took hold of his coat crying: "My lord! my lord! the curse of water!" but he wrenched himself away, and sprang into the boat. It was upset at the second wave of the Laufen, and both he and his friend were drowned; though often searched for, their bodies were never recovered.

Lady Cleveland, the present owner of the Battle Abbey, in a historical sketch, contributed to "Famous Homes of Great Britain," says: "On the open space in front the old bull-ring, still fixed in the ground, marks where the favorite Sussex sport of bull-baiting yearly went on in Whitsun week. To the west it is joined to a much older building, which retains one of its original Norman windows on the further side; to the east is a wing added by Lord Montagu as a Market House and Court Hall, probably in 1566, when he obtained an Act of Parliament for changing the weekly market from Sunday to Thursday. Its roof—no doubt long neglected—fell in during a great storm in 1764, and it is now a mere shell. The gateway contains a fine central hall reached by a carefully guarded staircase, that had not only a portcullis, but open spaces in its ribbed vaulting for pouring down boiling or melted lead on unwelcome visitors.

"The present entrance to the Abbey is not that originally in use, which was on the north side, where the offices now are, but leads through a porch into the Abbot's Hall. It is of noble proportions, measuring fifty-seven feet, both in height and in length, and thirty-one feet wide; with a fine timber roof, which, though modern, is a faithful copy of the ancient one taken down in 1812, and is of walnut wood grown in the park. All the oak wainscoting and carved work, as well as the great fireplace, were added by Sir Godfrey at the same time . . . . . . The stained glass is all heraldic; the south window showing the Duke's coat-of-arms, and some of the Paulet quarterings. Between the windows are ranged the shields and banners of the chief leaders in the Conqueror's army. [These would naturally include the equipments of Drogo de Montacute and Joscelyn de Bec]. Over the fireplace, two shields bear the arms of England and of the Abbey; and two banners display, one, the two lions or leopards of Normandy, the other, the gold cross on a silver field (figured in the Bayeux tapestry) of the consecrated banner sent to Duke William by the Pope. The coat and quarterings of the Viscounts Montagu are over the music gallery.

"Queen Elizabeth's wing left incomplete by Sir Anthony Brown (Montagu) is now occupied by a long and very handsome room, lighted by five great Tudor windows, three of them bays. Looking south and west, it is so flooded with sunshine that we had to guard it in the summer by our outer venetian blinds. It is entered from the hall through an ante-room built by the Duke, and contains the great library that he had been all his life collecting.

"There had always been a persistent tradition handed down from father to son, as to the place where King Harold was killed, and one particular spot on the turf was faithfully pointed out to sight-seers. At that time no one even guessed where the church had stood; generation after generation had passed away since its demolition; and if the waves of the sea had closed over it, it could scarcely have been more utterly lost. There were no indications of any kind to guide the explorer; but Sir Godfrey, wishing to test the truth of the tradition had the ground dug up,—and there, on the very spot it had been indicated, he found the high altar of the crypt, corresponding with that once in the chancel above! No historic locality could, I suppose be better ascertained or authenticated than this, marked out, immediately after the battle, by order of the Conqueror."

William Montagu, a direct descendant of Drogo de Montacute, married Margaret, daughter of John Malthouse, of Binfield, Berkshire, and had issue:

Peter Montague, married as already stated, Eleanor, daughter of William Allen, of Burnham, Bucks. They were the Parents of Peter Montague who settled in Virginia, and Richard, who settled in New England. One authority states, that: "It is known that they descended from the family of William Montagu, second Earl of Salisbury and eldest son of William, the first Earl, born June, 1328, eleventh descent from Drogo de Montagu."

Richard Montague, the first settler in New England of that name, son of Peter and Eleanor (Allen) Montague was born in Boveney about 1614. He came to New England, it is supposed, in 1634, and settled first in Salem, and moved thence to Wells, in what is now Maine but was then a part of the Massachusetts Bay Colony. In 1651 he moved to Wethersfield, Conn. It was not long after this that the divisions in the church took place and several of the members moved to Hadley, Mass., among them Richard Montague and his wife. When the attack was made on Hadley by the Indians he supplied the troops with food. He married Abigail Downing, daughter of Rev. Dr. Downing of Norwich, England. She also was of a very noted family, a descendant of some of the noblest families of England. His immediate ancestor was Sir Jeffrey Downing, married Elizabeth, daughter of Sir John Wingfield, whose family were famous for their Knighthood and ancient nobility. In his blood "says one authority," flows the commingled blood of Sir Simon Montague (A.D. 1300). William the

Conqueror, Malcolm, King of Scotland, William, Earl of Warren, William, Duke of Aquetaine, King Henry III., and other noble families.

This Richard Montague, by his wife Abigail (Downing) Montague, had issue

John Montague, born about 1655 in Wethersfield, Conn., and removed with his parents to Hadley,, Mass. in 1659. He married in Hadley, Hannah Smith, daughter of Chileah and Hannah (Hitchcock) Smith. On their tombstone is inscribed the following. "Ensign Chileah Smith died March 7, 1781, aged 96 years, and Hannah, his wife, died Aug. 31, aged 88 years. It is a worthy memorial that they lived in marriage state 70 years." They had ten children of whom was a son Richard.

Richard Montague, son of John and Hannah (Smith) Montague, was born in Hadley, Mass., March 10, 1684. He moved early in life to Withersfield, Conn., where he married, July 28, 1715, Abigail Camp. They were buried in the old cemetary at Withersfield, where their tombstones are still to be seen. They had issue John

John Montague, son of Richard and Abigail (Camp) Montague, was born in Wethersfield, Conn., Oct. 17, 1722. He married Sept. 27, 1759, Anna Belden. They were both admitted as members of the First Church of Wethersfield in 1751. They had issue Martha, born Nov. 15, 1754, married to Elisha Sage.

Elisha Sage by his wife Martha (Montague) Sage had issue

Rufus, born 1777.
Elisha Sage, born 1779 (See record below).
Martha, born 1781.
Barzello, " 1782.
Fanny, " 1784.
Molly, " 1785.
Mary, " 1787 (Woodworth).
Louisa, " 1789.
Amos, " 1791.
Calvin, " 1793.
Wealthy, " 1795 (Mooreson).
Cyprian, " 1801.

Elisha Sage (2), son of Elisha (1) and Martha (Montague) Sage, was born in Cromwell, (or Middletown Upper Houses) Conn., 1779, died 1854. He was an industrious hard working farmer, but he too, like his father and other ancestors had that strong love of country, the indomitable will and courage to overcome difficulties, and when he saw his country threatened by the same power against which his father and uncles had fought, he at once volunteered his services. He, like many others in Connecticut, had heard of the wonderful resources of the great West, and so he determined to leave the home of his childhood and erect a home for himself. Said a writer in the New York Times at the time of Russell Sage's death. "Elisha Sage was a man of parts. He had served through the war of 1812, and when he heard of the livelihood to be won by enterprises in the then unknown country, he packed his lodgings in an ox wagon and started out. He traversed the central part of New York and finally came to the little settlement of Shenandoah. There he stopped to rest, and his son Russell came into the world. The old house where this important event took place was torn down years ago, but the old barn attached to the place yet stands and has been used of late years as a tinker's shop." Elisha Sage settled in the township of Verona, in Oneida County, N. Y., in 1818, his intention at the time, being to go further west, but the birth of Russell decided him to settle in the township of Verona which had little more than a name at the time. He cleared the land and became a prosperous, well-to-do farmer. He married Prudence Risley.

Of the Risley family the History of Oneida County says: Capt. David Risley, a Revolutionary veteran, with his brothers Allen and Truman, settled very early south of New Hartford village, and west of what is now Washington Mills. They built a shanty and began making other improvements. Soon after his settlement, Capt. Risley built and opened a small store on his place. It was a log building, and he also built a log tavern which was a popular stopping place for travelers. Later he built a large frame store which soon became extensively patronized by the pioneers. He died August 24, 1834, aged 68 years. The children of Elisha and Prudence (Risley) Sage were

Henry R., born 1805.

Sallie, " 1807.

Fannie, " 1809.

Elisha M. and Elisha W., twins, born 1612.

William C., born 1814.

Russell Sage, born in Oneida County, N. Y., Aug. 4, 1816.

See record at the beginning of this work.

Part II. following contains the history of his wife's family (Margaret Olivia Slocum).

Errata.—Fifth line from the bottom should read Elisha M. and Elisha W., twins, born 1812.

Addenda

On page 41 it is stated that Lady Cleveland is still the owner of Battle Abbey. Mr. Michael B. Grace the present occupant of Battle Abbey (brother of ex-Mayor Grace of New York City), states in a letter to the author of this work that the Duchess of Cleveland died some six years ago. He states further that the Websters bought the place about 1730, and sold it to Lord Harry Vane, who became the Duke of Cleveland, It was left by will to his nephew Colonel Forrester who sold it to the present owner Sir Augustus Webster.

PART II.

THE SLOCUM, JERMAIN PIERSON AND ALLIED FAMILIES

Margaret Olivia Sage

THE SLOCUM AND ALLIED FAMILIES OF AMERICA

LINE OF MRS. MARGARET OLIVIA (SLOCUM) SAGE

THE name of Mrs. Margaret Olivia (Slocum) Sage, the widow of Russell Sage, has become almost as familiar to the American public as that of her distinguished husband. It requires greater wisdom, knowledge, tact and business sagacity to make a proper use of a large fortune than it does to acquire it. The demand is so great, and the avenues of its distribution are so numerous that it requires great discrimination, and taxes the mental faculties to their utmost capacity to know how to use it to the very best advantage. That this has been done by the possessor no one can doubt or gainsay.

Birth, education, environment, and a practical experience of many years along different lines have eminently qualified Mrs. Sage for this great responsibility and trust, and she has had opportunities for the indulgence of her tastes and inclinations that few women under like circumstances have enjoyed.

The public at large know little of the inner life of Mrs. Sage: this can only be judged by her works; and as these are largely of a public character it would be impossible for her to follow the scripture injunction: "Let not thy right hand know what thy left hand doeth"; and yet her own inclinations would naturally lead her to adopt such a course. From childhood up her whole life has been spent in promoting the happiness of those with whom she has been brought in contact, and a word of encouragement or sympathy from her has imparted renewed courage and strength to the depressed in spirit, who were struggling to overcome apparently insurmountable difficulties. Her old classmates, and the friends of her early years are, perhaps, the best judges of her true character, and their tributes of praise have been generously bestowed on one whom they delighted to honor. With the increased opportunities for doing good through the abundant means placed at her disposal, her friends were warm in their congratulations at this good fortune that enabled her to follow the promptings of her own generous heart. Many of them had enjoyed her confidence and knew of the high and pure motives that prompted every act of her life. It is from such sources as these that the writer has drawn his inspiration and gathered the facts relating especially to the personality of Mrs. Sage. No one can question the fact that the talents entrusted to her by an All-Wise Creator have multiplied at least an hundred fold; and that in the years to come thousands who have known her only by reputation will "rise up to call her blessed."

Those familiar with the life and characteristics of Mrs. Sage, as well as her educational religious and benevolent work will not fail to recognize in her the hereditary traits of her ancestors. One of these, Henry Pierson, brother of Rev. Abraham was the founder of the common school system of America, and was also a devout and earnest Christian. Governor Wanton, another ancestor, a native of Rhode Island who lived and practiced the simple life and faith of the Society of Friends, was one of the most refined and courteous men of his time, and had, it is said, the finest library in the colony of Rhode Island.

The strong personal traits, the independence, self-reliance and courage are clearly traceable to Capt. Myles Standish of the Mayflower. Her love of country, her patriotism, can be traced to her revolutionary ancestors, and the late Civil War furnished abundant evidence of the military spirit and heroism of the Slocums.

The origin of this family is clearly indicated by the construction of the name, and the compiler of the Slocum Genealogy states that it derives from a certain locality where there was an abundant growth of the Sloe; this being the fruit of the English wild spring Plum-tree, which is also known as the Sloe-tree, thorn and Black-thorn. The fruit was so named from its peculiar astringent action on the mouth known in English, as "setting the teeth on edge"; the primary significance of the word is harsh, blunt, dull, but this has no reference to family characteristics for the history of the family, both in the Old and New World indicates just the reverse of this description.

Efforts have been made to trace the family to its origin, and the compiler of the

Slocum Genealogy, states that the earliest record found by him was A. D. 1558, in Chatworthy, adjoining Huish Camflower. Capt. E. A. Lawson, a well known English genealogist discovered a Slocum will dated 1543, indicating that this surname must have existed at least as early as the fourteenth century. That some member of the family achieved distinction and was rewarded by his sovereign who conferred on him the coat armour is a well established fact. The same authority states that the Coat of Arms of the Slocombes of Somersetshire were seen by him in the British Museum Library, London, in the Harlein MS. No. 1385, which represents in part the report of the Herald's Visitation of Somersetshire England about the year 1573, described as

Arms—Argent on a fesse gules between three griffins' heads couped, sable, as many sinister wings, or.

Crest—A griffin's head gules between two wings expanded or.

Motto. Vivit post funera virtus. (Virtue outlives the grave.)

"Only the actions of the just
Look green and flourish in the dust."

In the Slocum Genealogy there is an illustrated representation of sprigs of the Sloe-tree in flower, leaf and fruit as signifying the origin of the name.

Wheeler's, in his "Reminescences of North Carolina," advances the theory that the derivation of the name of Slocum or Slocombe is from combe generally meaning a valley, but more literally cut-shaped depressions in hillsides, and sloe a kind of wild plum. It may have been that the first who received the surname of Slocombe, owned a combe or valley, noted for sloes, or lived near one; or perhaps from some noted person of the name of Combe, an ancient surname, wearing the leaves of the blackthorn or sloe as a badge or emblem, as the Earl of Anjou wore the sprigs of a broom, a badge or emblem of humility from which came the surname Broom in the Plantaganet royal family of England. The blackthorne or sloe, is an emblem of difficulty, and a sprig of it worn by the first Slocombes might mean "Valley men difficult to overcome, or hard to conquer."

A much more plausible and reasonable theory than either of the foregoing is that their name was originally Combe, and that a second or third son of a Combe who counted for little or nothing under the existing laws of primogenture, won distinction that entitled him to public recognition and, that living in a locality where the sloe grew in large quantities he was known as James or John Combe of the Sloe, and he was designated as the Sloe-Combe or Combe of the Sloe. The earliest records of the Slocombe family are found in Somersetshire, where one branch of the Combe family had long been seated. The earliest will of the Slocombes is dated 1543, which shows that the family must have had an existence under some other name at a much ealier period and that the surname of Slo-combe was adopted in the fifteenth century.

Whatever may have been their origin they were men of intellectual ability and high social standing as is evidenced by the descendants of the New England progenitors, many of whom have been conspicuous in civil and military life and have adorned the various professions which they entered.

It is claimed, and verified by the records that Anthony, Giles and Edward Slocombe came to New England about the same time and were the progenitors of most if not all the Slocums or Slocombes of this country. They were probably brothers, although the relationship has never been established. They probably all went first to the Plymouth Colony. Edward, the youngest, was in Taunton in 1643. He is mentioned in the Plymouth Colony Records, vol. I.—III. in June 1647, as one of the Supervisiors of Highways for Taunton. Giles and Edward probably both remained there, and while Anthony had lived in Taunton, his religious views and love of liberty, and his identity with the Society of Friends who were under the ban of the Plymouth authorities no doubt necessitated his removal to Rhode Island within the jurisdiction of the great-hearted, liberal-minded Roger Williams who gave a hearty welcome to the persecuted of every class, and Jew and Gentile, bond and free, were permitted to worship God under their own vine and fig tree with none to molest or make them afraid."

Anthony Slocum, the eldest, was one of the forty-six "first and ancient purchasers," A. D. 1637, of the territory of Cohannet, which was incorporated March 3d, 1639, with the name of Taunton in New Plymouth, and for which the present townships of Taunton, Raynham, and Berkeley have been organized. His name appears on the town records in various capacities as Surveyor of Highways and other positions. The place where he settled, near Pascamauset River, is more generally known as Slocum's River. The fragment of a letter written by his brother-in-law, without date, indicates that his wife was named Harvey.

"To the church of Christ in Taunton and the Shore [the pastor] and yourself in particular, I desire to be remembered, whose prayers, I doubt not, I and mine are the better for, and whose welfare I earnestly wish and pray for. Myself, wife and sons, and daughter, Gilbert, who hath four sons, remember our respects and loves, and my sons are all married. He had by his wife, Harvey, four children, of whom *Giles* was the eldest.

Giles Slocombe, eldest child of Anthony and (_______) Harvey Slocombe, was born in Somerset, England; he came to this country and settled in what is now the township of Taunton, New Plymouth, previous to 1675. Giles Slocum and his wife were early members of the Society of Friends. The Friends' records for Portsmouth, R. I., show that "Joan Slocum, the wife of old Giles, she Dyed at Portsmouth, the 31st 6 mo., 1670." He died in 1682. By his wife, Joan, he had seven children, of whom Peleg was the sixth.

Rev. Peleg Slocum, sixth child of Giles and Joan Slocum, was born in Portsmouth township, R. I., Jan. 17, 1654. He is named as one of the proprietors of Dartmouth in the confirmatory deed of Governor William Bradford, 13 Nov., 1694. In 1698 he and others "undertake to build a meeting-house for the people of God, in scorn called Quakers, 35 foot long, 30 foot wide, and 14 foot stud." Peleg Slocum's subscription, £15, was the largest on the list, and three times larger than any of the others, except John Tucker, who gave £10.

Peleg Slocum is recorded in the Friends' Records as a minister. Richardson in his Journal, 1701, wrote: "Peleg Slocum, an honest public Friend, carried us in his sloop to Nantucket.

Rev. Peleg Slocum married Mary Holder, daughter of Christopher Holder, born in Gloucester, England, in 1631; came to Boston, Mass., in 1656, and was there imprisoned and whipped, and his right ear cut off, as a punishment for being a Friend; "but he hearkened no better after these modes of persuasion, and flourished on transplantation to Providence, R. I., in 1665. He married Mary Scott, 12 Aug., 1660, daughter of Richard Scott and Catharine Marbury, who was the daughter of Edward Marbury, of Lincolnshire, England, Rector of St. Martin Vintry, London, who married Bridget Dryden, great aunt of Dryden, the famous poet. Mary Holder died Aug. 20, 1737, aged 75 years, 4 months and 14 days. Peleg Slocum had by his wife above-named ten children, of whom Joseph was the ninth.

Joseph Slocum, ninth child of Rev. Peleg and Mary (Holder) Slocum, was born March 13, 1701, in Dartmouth, Mass. He was admitted freeman of Newport, R, I., in 1722. He was named in his father's will, 13 June, 1731, as joint executor with his brother Holder; but in a letter dated at Newport, Feb. 5, 1732, he declined to act in that capacity, and requested Holder to assume entire control of the estate. He succeeded his father in the possession of Patience Island, in Narragansett Bay, R. I. He married, 1721, Susanna Wanton, of Newport, born 1704, daughter of Hon. John Wanton, who, as Savage states, "was chosen Governor of Rhode Island seven years, from 1733 to 1740.

Of this family John Russell Bartlett says: "Among the citizens of Rhode Island who have rendered distinguished service to the State since its foundation none are more prominent than the Wanton family. For a century their names appear among those who were prominent in social, political and commercial life. For several generations they were the leading merchants in the Colony. They were active in the support of religion, and in all works for the advancement of the interests of the town where they resided, as well as for the Colony at large. They were always found among the leaders. During the war between Great Britain and France, when two of them filled the office of Governor, they rendered distinguished service which was acknowledged by their sovereign. Four bearing the name were at different times elected Governor of the Colony—William Wanton, Governor in 1732, served two years; John, elected 1734, served seven years; Gideon, elected 1745, served two years; and Joseph, elected 1769, served until November, 1773. Another, Joseph, jr., held the office of Deputy-Governor. Portraits of William, John and Joseph are preserved in the Redwood Library, at Newport, and copies of the same have been placed in the State House in Providence."

Edward Wanton is the earliest ancestor of the family in this country. He was a resident of Boston, in 1658, and perhaps earlier. Tradition says he came from London accompanied by his mother, but of his father there is no record. It was quite a prominent family in England, and represented among the landed gentry.

The arms of the Wanton family are found on the tombstone of the wife of John Wanton [1720] in the old North Burying Ground at Newport, R. I.

Wanton.

Governor John Wanton [1734] and his son, Governor Gideon Wanton [1745], both of Rhode Island, used the same device on their official seals. These are the arms of the Wantons of County Huntington, England, described as:

Arms—Argent a chevron sable.

Crest—A plume of seven ostrich feathers; three argent, two sable, and two vert.

Motto—Mens sibi conscia recti (a mind conscious in itself of rectitude).

Edward Wanton was a resident of Scituate, Mass., in 1661, where he owned a farm of eighty acres at the well known ship-yard, a little below Dwelly's Creek. He had extensive lands in Cordwood Hill, and also at the southwest of Hoophole Hill. His house stood near the bank of the river. The persecution of the Friends (called in derision Quakers) by the authorities of the Massachusetts Bay Colony, influenced

Edward Wanton to join the Society. Deane, in his history of Scituate, says: "The severity of the Massachusetts Government toward this new sect had been carried on to the extent of executing three of them in 1659-60. Edward Wanton was an officer of the guard on one or more of these occasions. He became deeply sensible of the cruelty, injustice and impolicy of these measures, was greatly moved by the firmness with which they submitted to death, and was won entirely by their addresses before their execution. He returned to his house saying: "Alas, mother! we have been murdering the Lord's people;" and taking off his sword, but it by with a solemn vow never to wear it again. From this time he took every opportunity to converse with the Friends, and soon resolved to become a teacher of their faith." It is said that he built the first Quaker meeting-house in Massachusetts. He was most successful as a religious teacher in the Society of Friends. He died Oct. 16, 1716, aged 85, "with faculties unblurred, mind clear, piety fervent, faith unwavering, and active as he nearer approached its realization, from which standpoint he could review his past life, and with soul-stirring eloquence and deep sympathy exhort all to stand fast in the faith."

Soon after taking up his residence in Scituate, Mr. Wanton received a visit from a Quaker preacher, recently arrived from England, who recommended to him as a second wife a woman in that country with whom he was well acquainted. After a brief correspondence between the two, the lady came to America in 1663. They were married, and lived happily together. They had issue, Joseph, born 1664; George, 1666; Elizabeth, William, 1670; John, 1672; Sarah and Margaret, twins, 1674; Michael, 1679; Stephen, 1682; Philip, 1686.

Governor John Wanton, fifth son of Edward, was born in 1672. In consequence of religious differences in the family, some of the members being connected with the Episcopal Church and others with the Society of Friends, John and his brother William moved to Newport, Rhode Island, where they carried on a large and successful business as shipping merchants.

John Wanton first appears in public life as a Deputy to the General Assembly from Newport in 1706, where he is styled "Captain." Two years later he is styled "Colonel," at which time he was commander of a regiment of militia, and accompanied the famous expedition to Canada.

During the war with France news was brought to Newport that a ship laden with provisions had been captured by a French privateer off Block Island. A proclamation, calling upon the inhabitants for volunteers, was at once issued by Colonel Cranston. Within two hours time two sloops were armed, equipped and manned with one hundred and twenty men, and placed under the command of Colonel John Wanton, who immediately put to sea. They soon fell in with the Frenchman, whom they captured, and within twelve hours from their departure, they entered the harbor with the privateer and the sloop she had previously taken. This was one of the greatest feats recorded in naval warfare of that period.

After many years of active life connected with military and naval enterprises, Colonel Wanton, about 1712, laid aside all warlike aspirations and joined the Society of Friends. He had been a most successful merchant, and was considered the wealthiest man in the Colony. The good use he made of his riches in acts of benevolence, and his devotion to his country, obtained for him a popularity such as no citizen of the Colony had ever before acquired.

From 1712 to 1721 he was among the Deputies or Assistants to the General Assembly from Newport until 1721, when he was elected Deputy-Governor, and re-elected, and in 1729 was elected Governor, and continued in office for seven years.

He was a liberal patron of the arts, collected a fine library and some philosophical apparatus. His home was the intellectual centre of the Colony, and the fame of his library and apparatus extended throughout the neighboring colonies, so that when strangers visited the town his home was one of the desirable places to visit; and he was like his brothers, very hospitable, refined, instructive in conversation, possessing those elegancies of manner which distinguished the gentlemen of his day. He died May 5, 1744. He married, first, Ann, daughter of Gideon Freeborn, of Portsmouth, R. I. He married, secondly, Mary Stafford, of Swinton. His daughter, Susanna, born 1704, was married to Joseph Slocum.

Joseph Slocum, by his wife, Susanna (Wanton) Slocum, had three children, of whom John was the youngest.

John Slocum, youngest child of Joseph and Susanna (Wanton) Slocum, was born May 5, 1727, in or near the village of Newport. He was a prosperous farmer, and lived a quiet, uneventful life. He married Hannah, daughter of William Brown and Rebecca (Lawton) Brown.

"William Brown and Rebeckah Lawton married by John Wanton, Governor, Dec. 10, 1734."

William Brown was the son of Tobias Brown, son of William, son of Nicholas Brown, one of the early settlers of Portsmouth, R. I. He was probably the son of Nicholas Brown, of Lynn, Mass.

Nicholas Brown, the ancestor of this branch of the Brown family, was of Lynn, Mass., as early as 1630 or 1637. He was the son of Edward Brown, of Inkberrow, eight miles from Droitwich, Worcestershire, England. He was admitted freeman of the Massachusetts Bay Colony in 1638. He was a Representative to the General Court of Massachusetts from Lynn, 1641. He removed to Reading, Mass., in 1644. He died April 5, 1673.

Nicholas Brown, of Portsmouth, R. I., 1638, was probably a son of Nicholas, of Lynn, Mass. He was admitted an inhabitant of the island of Aquedneck. The Rhode Island Colony Records state that in 1639 "Nicholas Brown doth disarm himself of the government here."

"April 30, 1639, he and twenty-eight others signed the following agreement or compact: 'We, whose names are underwritten, do acknowledge ourselves the legal subjects of King Charles, and in his name do bind ourselves into a civil body of politicke unto his laws according to matters of Justice.'"

He married Frances Parker, widow of George Parker, of Portsmouth, 1638, who came from London in 1635, in the "Elizabeth and Ann," aged 23. He was serg.-gen. He died in 1656, leaving a widow. He had twenty-nine acres to his other twenty acres adjoining. His children by Frances (Parker) Brown were:

Nicholas.

Abraham.

Jane, born 1677.

William Brown. (See record.)

His will, dated Nov. 10, 1694, proved Dec. 27, 1694, names Executor, grandson, Tobias; to his eldest son he gives 5s.; to his daughter, Jane Babcock, £10; to granddaughters, Martha and Jane Brown, daughters of son, William, deceased, each £10; to grandson, Tobias, son of William, all my lands and houses in Rhode Island, and all neat cattle, sheep, horsekind and hogs, carts, plows, corn, hay, pewter, brass, iron, provision, apparel and bedding.

William Brown, youngest son of Nicholas and Frances (Parker) Brown, was born in Portsmouth, R. I., about 1679. He appears to have been the favorite child, as he is named in his father's will as the principal legatee. "All my houses and property in Rhode Island" indicates that he would have been a man of considerable wealth for that day, had he lived; but he died before his father. He had a son, Tobias, and other children.

Tobias Brown, son of William Brown, was born in Portsmouth, R. I., about 1679; died, 1734. He married Alice Buovington, and had issue.

John, born 1705.

William Brown, born 1709. (See record.)

Sarah, born 1713.

Nicholas.

Robert.

Alice.

William Brown, second child of Tobias and Alice (Buovington) Brown, was born in Portsmouth, R. I., in 1711. He married Rebekah Lawton, born April 25, 1711, daughter of Isaac and Elizabeth (Talman) Lawton, son of George Lawton, one of the early proprietors of Portsmouth, R. I. They had issue, Hannah and other children.

Hannah Brown, daughter of William and Rebeckah (Lawton) Brown, was born in Portsmouth, R. I., June 23, 1735; married June 20, 1754, to John Slocum.

John Slocum, by his wife, Hannah (Brown) Slocum, had issue:

I. John, born Dec. 20, 1759; married Phebe Durfee.

II. Peleg, born 1765; married Hannah Stoddard.

III. Mary, born 4th May, 1767.

IV. William Brown Slocum, born 26 April, 1770. (See record below.)

Hon. William Brown Slocum, youngest child of John and Hannah (Brown) Slocum, was born in Middleton, Newport County, R. I., April 20, 1770. He married Olivia Josselyn, of Stockbridge, Mass., April 28, 1793. Soon after his marriage he moved to Rensselaer County, N. Y., where he cultivated a large farm, and was also a dealer in live stock. He took an active and prominent part in the public affairs of State and County, and in 1820-21 was elected to the State Assembly. This was at a period in the history of the Empire State when it was an honor to fill such a position; when men of intellectual worth and influence—statesmen rather than politicians—were sent to represent their districts in the councils of the State. It was at a period when Erie Canal and other great public enterprises formed the leading topics of discussion, and occupied the attention of the State Legislature. His contemporaries and co-workers were the Clintons, the Van Rensselaers, the Livingstons, and other men of that stamp, who laid the foundations of our commercial prosperity through wise legislation and public addresses, Mr. Slocum had a share in all this, and helped to shape the destinies of his adopted State. Both his public and private life were exemplary in the highest degree. He enjoyed a personal popularity, due to his many noble and manly qualities. He died at Speigletown, Rensselaer County, New York, May 29, 1823, and was buried at that place. His widow died in Lansingburgh, N. Y., greatly beloved and honored by all who knew her. No higher tribute could be paid to any woman than the sentiments expressed in the inscription on her tombstone: "Her's was a piety deep in its veins, and holy and most benignant in its influence." Through Mary Holder she was descended from the Drydens, closely related to Dryden the

Olivia Josselyn Slocum
(Mrs. William Brown Slocum)

poet. She was a woman of culture, refinement and deep religious nature. She evinced the poetic genius of the Drydens, as shown in the following lines, which, through a custom in those days of "sampler" needle-work, have been preserved to posterity:

Let piety, celestial guest,
With wisdom flourish in my breast;
And virtue, lovely, heavenly, fair,
Hold an unrivaled impress there.
Let living faith and love divine,
Possess this youthful heart of mine;
That when my flesh returns to dust,
My soul may triumph with the just.

Olivia Josselyn was the daughter of Stockbridge Josselyn and Olivia Standish. Stockbridge Josselyn was the son of Thomas, son of Henry, son of Abraham, son of Thomas Josselyn, the ancestor of this branch of the Josselyn family.

She was married to Hon. William Slocum, April 28, 1793. Their daughter, L. Josselyn Slocum, worked the above in her "sampler," a beautiful piece of needlework of that period.

JOSSELYN OR JOCELYN FAMILY

This is a noted and very ancient family, settled in Kent and Essex Counties, England. One of the most prominent representatives of the family was

Sir Ralph Jocelyn, K. B., who was lineally descended, through the marriage of Thomas Jocelyn with Maud, daughter and co-heir of Sir John Hyde, from Sir Gilbert de Jocelyn, one of the companions in arms of the conqueror. This Sir Ralph was Sheriff of London in 1458, and Lord Mayor in 1464. In 1467 Sir Ralph represented the City of London in Parliament, and was again Lord Mayor in 1476. His portrait and also the portrait of his wife, whose second name was Barley, and her second husband, Sir Robert Clifford, Knt., are in Medford Church, Suffolk, in perfect glass, of the date about 1490.

The Horseley and Newhall Jocelins were seated in County Essex, while another branch of Jocelyn, or Jocelyne, were seated at Sawbridgeworth, County Hertford. All were descended, however, from the same family.

The armorial bearings of the New England family of Josselyns as described by Barry, in his History of Hanover, Mass., were:

Arms—Chequy gules and azure, on a fesse of the first, an annulet, or,

Crest—A bear's head and neck, sable muzzled, or,

Motto—Fain mon devoir (To do my duty.)

Barry says further: "In America John Josselyn, gent., was in New England in 1638, and was the author, among other works, of one called New England's Rarities, and Henry, his brother (and son of Sir Thomas, of Kent), was at Black Point, now Scarborough, Me., in 1634, being sent out by Capt. Mason to make a more complete discovery and examination of the advantages of the grant made to Capt. Mason. He was a member of the General Court at Saco, in 1636; Councillor, 1639; Deputy-Governor, 1648; a magistrate and member of the government of the province of Ligonia during in 1650; a commissioner and associate under Massachusetts, 1658; and the long period, from 1635 to 1676, he was one of the most active and influential men in the Province; and during all the changes of proprietorship and government he held the most important offices. He married Margaret, widow of Capt. Thomas Cammot, and it is said had one son, Henry. Family tradition and other authorities assert that this son settled in Scituate, Mass., in 1668; married Abigail Stockbridge in 1678, and was the ancestor of the Josselyns of Plymouth County, Mass."

According to Massachusetts Historical Collections, 3d Series, Vol. viii., Thomas Josselyn, a husbandman, aged 43, Rebecca, his wife, of the same age, and their children, Rebecca, aged 18; Dorothy, aged 11; Nathaniel, aged 8; Eliza, aged 6; and Mary, aged 1, with a maid servant, Eliza Ward, aged 36, came to New London in the Increase, of London, Robert Lea, master, in 1635; and, according to Lincoln's History of Hingham, Thomas, the father, was in Hingham in 1637, and in 1652 he was in Lancaster (Worcester Mag. II., 280), where he died in 1660 (Middlesex Record), his widow, Rebecca, being executrix of his estate. She married William Kelsey in 1664.

Abraham Josselyn, son of Thomas, the ancestor, had an assignment of land in Hingham, Mass., in 1647. He did not come with his father in the Increase, but at a later period. In the summer of 1660 the birth of his son, Nathaniel, was recorded in Boston. He removed to Lancaster before 1663, and died there July 9, 1670; where "William Kirby, of Marlborough, husbandman, by the consent and approbation of

Abbey du Bec

Near Brionne, Normandy, France---a portion of the Josselin Estate

The first illustration represents the location and a portion of the remains of Abbey du Bec, which comprised a part of the original Castle of Teustan du "Bec" or as he was known Gilbertus (Galfridus) Josselinus. This property was inherited by him from his father. The other illustrations represent the exterior and interior of the Josselin salon as it appears at the present time. This Teustan du Bec accompanied William the Conqueror to England where his name is inscribed in the Roll of Battle Abbey.

Dr. Ducarel in his Norman Antiquities (1767) says: "This famous Benedictine Abbey du Bec, or, as it is generally known Bec Hillouin, stands near Brionne about nine miles distant from Caen, and is situated in a narrow vale, enclosed by two steep mountains, along the foot of which runs a small brook, known as le Bec which rises out of the adjacent mountain. This Abbey was founded about 1034 by Hillouin, a noble Dane. A few years after its completion a great part of the building fell down; and Saufranc, the Prior of the monastery, afterwards Archbishop of Canterbury induced Hillouin to erect a new one, which was completed in 1073. The noble founder amply endowed it, and procured therewith grants of many extensive and valuable privileges and exemptions, all of which were afterward confirmed by the French Kings, as also Henry I., Henry II., John, Henry III., Stephen and Henry V., Kings of England.

The present Abbey Church (1763) which was begun in 1273, on the same spot where the old one was destroyed by fire, in 1264, is justly esteemed one of the finest Gothic churches in France.

"In the front there are two noble columns of jasper, whose pedestals and capitals are of the finest statuary marble. All the metopes are of jasper, and over them are placed the figures of several utensils belonging to the temple of Solomon. The ark of the covenant stands over the middlemost metope, and on each side are alternately placed the table of shew-bread, the altar of incense and the attributes of the evangelists. Within the tympan, or panel of the pediment is a basso relievo of mital, representing Adam and Eve standing at the foot of the tree of Knowledge in the attitude of the strongest contrition and deploring the sin which they had just committed."

Of the remains of the old Abbey the church is best preserved and also some fine statues and beautiful enamels. The rest of the buildings have been turned into a Military Station for cavalry mounts.

Abbey du Bec

Chateau de Josselin—Facade sur l'Oust

Chateau de Josselin—Le Salon

Mrs. Beatris Joscelyn, the late decd. Abram Joceline's widow, sold to Abram Jocelin, eldest son of the late Mrs. Jocelin, 86 acres of land in Lancaster."

The name of Abraham Josselyn's wife, Beatrice, is variously written Beatris, Beatrix and Betteris. In Middlesex Deeds (iii., 15) is the following: "Abram Joslin, of Lancaster, and his wife, Betteris, sold on the 29th of May, 1663, to Henry Kemble, of Boston, certain lands in Lancaster, formerly granted to his (Abraham's) father, Thomas Joslin."

By his wife, Beatrice, Abraham Josselyn had issue:

I. Abraham, bap. at Hingham April 8, 1649.

II. Philip, bap. Dec. 15, 1650.

III. Nathaniel, bap. July 4, 1660.

IV. Joseph, born at Lancaster, May 21, 1663.

V. Mary, born Oct. 14, 1666.

VI. Henry Josselyn, date of birth not found (see record).

VII. Rebecca " " " " "

Henry Josselyn, youngest son of Abraham and his wife, Beatrice, was born in Lancaster, Mass., about 1668-70. He was in Scituate as early as 1669. The Court Records show that Henry Josselyn, of Scituate, and his wife, Abigail, sold, Nov. 1, 1695, to Thomas Hurns, of Boston, 110 acres of land in Lancaster. His house stood stood in the field, 50 rods east of Judge William Cushing's farm. He died in Hanover, Mass., Oct. 30, 1739, being called on the Church Records " the oldest man in the town for years." He married Abigail Stockbridge, daughter of Deacon Charles Stockbridge, who gave the silver communion cups to the Church. The records state that " the church received a present of four silver cups for the communion table by order and at the expense of Deacon Stockbridge; the cost of cup at £25 old tenor." He was the son of John Stockbridge, who came to New England in the Blessing, in 1635, being then 27 years of age.

The Stockbridge was a knightly family, early seated in Huntingdonshire, and had for armorial bearings:

Arms—Argent on a chevron azure, three crescents, or

Crest—Out of a cloud two dexter hands in armour conjoined, holding up a heart inflamed all proper.

Charles Stockbridge, before mentioned (son of John), is said to have built, by contract, the second water mill in the town of Plymouth, in 1676. He died in 1683, and his widow married Amos Turner. His second child, Abigail, born at Charlestown, Mass., Feb. 24, 1660, was married to Henry Josselyn.

Henry Josselyn, by his wife, Abigail (Stockbridge) Josselyn, had issue:

I. Abigail, born 1677, married Dec. 15, 1715, Benjamin Hammer.

II. Abraham, born January, 1678-9.

III. Ann, born February, 1680.

IV. Charles, born March, 1682.

V. Mary, born January, 1684.

VI. Nathaniel, born February, 1686.

VII. Rebecca, born — —, died 1689.

VIII. Jabez, born February, 1690.

IX. Rebecca, born May, 1693; married April 24, 1778, Jos. Perry.

X. Jemima, born December, 1695; died February, 1696.

XI. Keziah, born December, 1695.

XII. Henry, born March, 1697.

XIII. Joseph, born December, 1697; married Ruth Bates. He was known as Capt. Joseph Josselyn, and was a man of much influence and great prominence in the community. He served in the French and Indian war.

XIV. Thomas Josselyn, born September, 1703 (see record).

Thomas Josselyn, youngest child of Henry, by his wife, Abigail (Stockbridge) Josselyn, was born in 1702. He was known as Deacon Thomas Josselyn. He was quite active in church, also in public affairs, and his is the only name in the town mentioned in connection with one of the most notable events in connection with the history of the Massachusetts Colony, viz.:

In 1740 a company was enlisted in the county of Plymouth, by Capt. Winslow, to serve in the expedition against the Spanish West Indies, under Admiral Vernon. Of the 500 men sent by Massachusetts, not more than 50 returned; but their arrival in Havana led to the capture of that stronghold by the British.

The Town Records, under date of Dec. 28, 1741, contain the following: "Voted Deacon Thomas Josselyn £13 16s. 4d. for men's rates to Cuba and elsewhere." The names of those who went from Hanover are not given.

The church records of Hanover contain the following relative to a gift of Deacon Thomas Josselyn:

"July 8, 1786, two silver cups for the communion table were received, a legacy from Deacon Thomas Josselyn to perpetuate the memory of the benefactor."

In referring to the new church erected in 1764, it is stated that the spire of this house was removed about 1784, when a bell was presented to to the society by Mr. Josselyn.

Thomas Josselyn married June 1, 1732, Jane Stockbridge (born May 31, 1710), daughter of Thomas Stockbridge, who is called on the Church Records Ensign Thomas. He was the son of Charles, son of John Stockbridge, the ancestor. The children of of Thomas Josselyn, by his wife, Ann (Stockbridge) Josselyn, were:

I. Thomas, born September 26, 1733; married Patience Baker.

II. John, born May 4, 1735.

III. Ann, or Nancy, born October 3, 1736; died April 21, 1801.

IV. Stockbridge Josselyn, born April 29, 1741 (see record).

V. Ruth, born January, 1745.

VI. Deborah, born 1752.

VII. Philip, born 1754.

VIII. Isaiah.

IX. Seth; married Priscella Standish, December 17, 1787.

Stockbridge Josselyn, fourth child of Thomas and Ann (Stockbridge) Josselyn, was born March 29, 1741; died May 10, 1817, aged 76. He married, November 24, 1768, Olivia Standish, daughter of David and Hannah (Magoun) Standish, son of Thomas and Mary (Carver) Standish, son of Alexander and Desire (Doty, etc.) Standish, son of Capt. Myles Standish, of the Mayflower (see Standish family).

THE STANDISH FAMILY OF ENGLAND.

The history of the Standish family begins early in the eleventh century, previous to the reign of Henry III., and more than five hundred years before Capt. Myles Standish, the great military head of the Plymouth Colony, made his appearance.

The following pedigree is compiled from an abstract of the charter and muniments of Standish, drawn up by Rev. Thomas West, domestic chaplain of the Strickland family, author of the *History of Furness Abbey*. The first record found by him is that of

—— De Standish, who had married Margaret, daughter and co-heir of Robert de Hulton, became, in her right, possessed of the manor of Shevington. Of the Hultons a well-known authority says: "This family possesses the most unerring proof of antiquity in the title deeds of their estate of Hulton, from which the Hultons derive their surname, and of which they have been uninterrupted lords since the Conquest." The first de Standish, by his wife, Margaret Hulton, had a son and successor.

Thurston de Standish, who, 4 Feb., 6th Henry III., anno. 1221, levied a fine of lands in Shevington, which he inherited from his mother, Margaret, daughter and co-heir of Robert de Hulton. He was living in the 20th of the same reign, A.D. 1225-36, and had a son,

Ralph de Standish, who had two sons, viz.: Jordan, his successor, and Hugh.

Hugh Standish, son of Ralph, was the founder of the Duxbury Park (county Lancaster) family. He married (34 Edward I.) Alice, daughter of Sir Richard Molyneux, of Sefton, in Lancashire, and had two sons, William Standish, who died young, and

Richard Standish, of Duxbury, living 9th Edward III.; he was the father of two sons, Hugh and John.

Hugh Standish, of Duxbury, married, in 1639, his kinswoman, Alice, daughter of Henry Standish, of Standish. [This Henry de Standish, who, on the death of his brother, Sir Ralph, recovered the family estates, was the son of John de Standish, Lord of Standish, son of William de Standish, son of Jordan de Standish, brother of Hugh de Standish, the founder of the Duxbury branch, and son of Ralph.] The only surviving son of Hugh Standish, of Duxbury, was

Christopher Standish, of Duxbury; married (9th Richard II.) Margaret, daughter of Sir Thomas Fleming, and had issue:

Ralph, who married (7th Henry V.) Joan, daughter of Sir Thomas Gerard, Knt.

Rowland (Sir), who received the honor of knighthood, 19th Henry V. He brought the riches of St. Lawrence from Normandy to Chorley Church.

James, the continuator of the family.

James Standish, of Duxbury, youngest son of Christopher Standish, had, by his wife, Alice,

Christopher Standish, Esq., of Duxbury, whose son,

Sir Christopher Standish, of Duxbury, knighted by Richard III. He married, and had issue: Thomas, James, Hugh, Alexander, Rowland, Anne, and Maud, wife of William Braidshaigh, Esq., of Haigh. The eldest son,

Thomas Standish, Esq., of Duxbury, married, in 1497, Catharine, daughter of Sir Alexander Standish, of Standish (Knighted at Hulton-Field in 1482), by Sibella, his wife, daughter of Henry Bold, Esq., of Bold, in Lancashire, and had a son and successor,

James Standish, Esq., of Duxbury, who married, first, Elizabeth, daughter of Ewen Hadock, and, secondly, Elizabeth, daughter of John Butler, Esq., of Rawcliffe. He was succeeded by his son,

Thomas Standish, Esq., of Duxbury, who married Margaret, daughter of Sir Thomas Hoghton, in Lancashire, and was succeeded by his son,

Alexander Standish, Esq., of Duxbury, father, by Margaret, his wife, daughter of Sir Ralph Asheton, Bart., of Whaley Abbey, of several children. The eldest son,

Thomas Standish, Esq., of Duxbury, married, first, Anne, eldest daughter of Sir Thomas Wingfield, Knt., of Letheringham, in Suffolk, and had by her, Thomas, Alexander, Richard, Anne, and Ratclyffe. He married, secondly, Anne, daughter of Christopher Whittingham, Esq., of Suffolk, by whom he had Ralph, Gilbert, Henry, Catharine, Margaret, and Dorothy. Thomas, the eldest son, was slain at Manchester by the parliamentarians, dying without issue; the line was continued through Richard, the youngest son of Thomas, by his wife, Anne Wingfield, down to the eighteenth century. The following are the armorial bearings of the Duxbury family:

Arms—Azure, three standishes argent.

Crest—A cock argent.

Motto—Constant en tout.

Seat—Duxbury Park, Lancashire, and Cocken Hall, Durham.

A well known authority (Vermont) says: Capt. Miles Standish descended from Thurston de Standish. The branch of Duxbury, county Lancaster, from which the emigrant descended, originated with Hugh Standish (temp. Edward I.), and adopted the reformed religion.

The records of the parish of *Chorley*, with which the family estate is connected, were examined some years since by the agents of the American Standishes, and it is said that "these records were easily deciphered, with the exception of the years 1584 and 1585, the very dates about which Capt. Myles Standish is supposed to have been born; the parchment-leaf which contained the register of both of these years being wholly illegible, and showing evident traces of having been tampered with."

THE LINE OF CAPT. MYLES STANDISH
OF THE PLYMOUTH COLONY
SHOWING THE CONNECTION WITH THE SLOCUM FAMILY

Capt. Myles Standish was born, as is supposed, about 1584. He was a soldier from his youth up.

"A stouter champion never handled sword,
Long since we were resolved of your truth,
Your faithful service, and your toil in war."

His first military service was during the reign of Queen Elizabeth, from whom he received a commission in the English army in Holland, then aiding the Dutch against Spain.

His Christian name, Myles, is an old Roman name for soldiers. He is described as "short of stature," but he certainly was "long in reach" and powerful in stroke whenever he wielded that trusty blade in defence of a righteous cause. He was not a devout man in religion by any means, and his life in Leyden with the Pilgrims was that of a casual defender of religious liberty, rather than a "soldier of the cross." He certainly was a great acquisition to the little colony that set sail on the Mayflower, Aug. 21, 1620, having abandoned the Speedwell, which started sixteen days earlier, but, having been reported as leaky, was abandoned for the former. With Capt. Standish came his wife, Rose, who died the following year.

Stern of purpose, a disciplinarian in the broadest sense of the word, always a leader as trouble confronted them; a man bristling with danger signals when aroused, he yet has given to history the most romantic side of all the colonists.

High of station, free from care, holding a military position, he was fully in accord with, his joining the little band was a mystery; but he was a zealous, devoted citizen, one with them in all thought and deed save the very purpose which made their exile bearable.

The freedom to worship God according to the dictates of their own consciences had little interest for him. Some historians declare him to have been of the Catholic faith of his fathers. From this he certainly changed with change of environment, but he always retained his independence of action, and would brook no restraint from any source, being answerable only to his own conscience for his method of religious service.

On the 21st of November, after a passage of sixty-six days, the Mayflower dropped anchor in Cape Cod harbor. "Like the down of the thistle they were wafted across the sea, and the seed they bore of popular government and religious freedom was planted on those western shores."

On the 11th day of December (old style) the exploring party of Pilgrims, who had left their ship, the Mayflower, in Cape Cod harbor, landed at Plymouth, where they found "a place (as they supposed) fitt for the situation; at least it was ye best they could find, and ye season and their presente necessities made them glad to accept of it. So they returned to their shippe again with this news to ye rest of their people, which did much comfort their harts."

On the same day of this report the first civil act of the Pilgrims was to draw up a Compact, or "combination," as Bradford calls it, which was signed by the male members of the company, and became the foundation on which the structure of our government has been built. There were 41 signers to to this "Compact," and from 1 to 7 they appear in the following order, apparently according to procedure: The first is John Carver; 2, William Bradford; 3, Edward Winslow; 4, Elder William Brewster; 5, Isaac Allerton; 6, Myles Standish; 7, John Alden.

Born, as it is asserted, in 1584, Myles Standish, it was found by the association formed in 1846 to endeavor to regain the estate belonging to him in England, held the commission of Lieutenant, given him by Queen Elizabeth. As he is first mentioned as Captain, that is probably the rank he bore when he left Leyden.

The familiar story of his courtship by proxy of Priscilla Molines is familiar to every New England descendant, and he probably yielded gracefully to the inevitable. There is no evidence of any resentment to the successful suitor of Priscilla's hand, and she set an example to the leap-year maidens when she said: "Why not ask for yourself, John?"

Oliver Wendell Holmes, in his "Landing a Punch Bowl," has fully described the man, when he says:

"'Twas on a dreary winter's eve; the night was closing dim,
When brave Myles Standish took the bowl and filled it to the brim:
The little captain stood and stirred the posset with his sword,
And all his sturdy men-at-arms were ranged about the board."

This sword referred to, with its Arabic inscription, of which he was so justly proud, was fit for all occasions, whether to "stir the posset" or to carve a turkey. The inscription on this sword is thus translated: "With peace God ruled His slaves" (meaning creatures), "and with the judgment of His arm He troubled the mightly of the wicked" (meaning the most powerful and evil of the wicked).

He wielded this sword with terrible effect on the Indians, the inveterate foe of the white man. The Indians, without civilization and its consequent tempering, made repeated attacks on the unprotected settlers, but they soon learned to fear the white man's "Protector." One Indian who, with the cunning of his savage nature, made a trade in furs an excuse for an interview, but returned to his tribe not the least deceived by the calm demeanor of the Captain, informed them that "he saw by his eye that he (Standish) was angry in his heart."

He stood at all times between the people and the dangers that surrounded them. He did not go with the "sword in one hand and an olive branch in the other." Upon his foresight, grasp of the situation and decisive action, depended the very existence of the colony. Prompt measures alone would serve as an example.

He simply obeyed orders, was true to his oath of office, conforming to the "blue book" of the day, which then, as now, left no alternative of action. Pastor Robinson, one of his warmest friends, was wont "to consider the disposition of their captain, who was warm of temper." In his will Standish remembered "Mayre Robinson, in consideration of the love he bore her grandfather."

He conducted all the early expeditions against the Indians, and continued in the military service of the Colony during his whole life. He commanded the Plymouth troops which marched against the Narragansetts in 1645; and when hostilities with the Dutch were apprehended, in 1653, he was one of the Council of War, of Plymouth, and was appointed to command the troops which the Council determined to raise.

He was also prominent in the civil affairs of the Colony. He was for many years Assistant, or a member of the Governor's Council; and when, in 1626, it became necessary to send a representation to England to represent the colonists in their business arrangements, he was selected, and entrusted with full power to act.

The need of room, perhaps a desire for a change of privileges, about 1630, sent the Pilgrims to Duxbury, "close by," which was so named after the English home of the Standish family. The following, from the town records, indicate the cause, perhaps the principal one, for the change:

"Ano. 1632, April 2. The names of those which promise to remove their families to live in the towne in the winter time, that they may the better to the worship of God:

John Alden,
Capt. Standish,
Jonathan Brewster,
Thomas Prence.

Capt. Standish showed his strength of character by using, not abusing, his power; and strange as it may appear, though his intercourse with the Indians was of the law and order style, they appreciated the position he took, that he was their just friend in reverses, and rendered him affection and even homage in many instances.

The Indian, Hobomok, who was a friend of the English, early adopted the Christian religion, and became an inmate of Capt. Standish's home, endearing himself to all by his loyalty, going with Standish as his guide and interpreter. According him the spirit and power of a ruler, the quick resentment that had a code of honor where wrongs were inflicted, the records of Plymouth and Duxbury hold no cleaner pages than those which bore his name, telling that he only twice appeared before the Court, and then simply to punish offenders for cruelty to his animals; once his dog.

"Though small of stature, he had an active genius, a sanguine temper, and a strong constitution," affording us "an instance not only of the nerve of the Pilgrims, but a type of their hearts." He "died Oct. 31, 1650, aged 72," a man full of years, and honored by his generation. By his wife, Barbara, who probably came in the Ann, in 1625, he had issue:

Alexander Standish (see record below).
Charles, living 1627.
John, "
Myles, died April 5, 1663.
Josiah, " March 7, 1690.
Lord

Alexander Standish, eldest child of Capt. Myles Standish and Barbara Standish, his wife, was born probably about 1623, and was admitted freeman of the Colony, 1648. He was clerk of Duxbury 1695-1700. Referring to church arrangements in the settlement at Duxbury, it is said that "when the distance being great, they were obliged to have a meeting-house of their own, in due course of time, Alexander Standish, always the heir-apparent, was deacon."

Alexander Standish married, first, Sarah, daughter of John Alden, and by her had seven children.

He married, secondly, Desire, first the widow of Israel Holmes, and second, that of William Sherman. Her maiden name was Doty, and she was the daughter of Edward Doty.

Edward Doty came in the Mayflower in 1620, a London youth in the service of Stephen Hopkins, and was the Fortieth Signer of the Mayflower Compact. Regarding his ancestral line and social standing at home, a careful research was made in 1873 by Albert G. Welles, President of the Genealogical Society, and M. S. Foreman, the Secretary, and as the result, stated Edward Dotey, or Doughty, of the Mayflower, was an English youth belonging to the same family as Sir Charles Montague Doughty, or Doty, of Therburton Hill, Suffolk County, England, formerly of Lincoln County.

This family has an ancient and honorable record that dates back to the Norman Conquest.

There is a well founded statement in writing that "Edward Doty ran away from home in resentment of his oldest brother's inheritance of the home and emoluments," has not only a foundation in truth, but there is more to it than this fact. Under the law of primogeniture introduced by Norman lawyers soon after the Norman Conquest, only the eldest son had any rights, and the younger son, in common with all others, under the laws of England, was obliged to serve his apprenticeship of seven years to earn the rights of citizenship. This was Edward Doty's situation when he entered the service of Stephen Hopkins and occupied the same position socially at that of any other member.

Edward Doty completed his apprenticeship and by 1640 he was a considerable land owner and a man of position and influence. He married 1634-1635, Fayth Clarke only 16 years of age, daughter of Thurston Clarke. It is said that she had a very beautiful home at Plymouth on the "High Cliff" when the following named children were born, Edward, John, Desire Doty, (see record), Samuel Thomas, Elizabeth, Isaac, Joseph and Henry.

Desire Doty, third child of Edward and Faith (Clarke) Doty, after being twice married, and twice a widow became the wife of Alexander Standish.

Alexander Standish by his wife Desire nee Doty had issue

Thomas Standish, born 1687, (See record).

Desire, born 1689.

Ichabod.

David.

Thomas Standish, eldest child of Alexander and Desire (Sherman nee Doty) Standish was born 1687. He married Mary Carver, daughter of William, son of John, son of Robert, one of the early settlers of Marshfield and brother of Govenor John Carver.

William Carver, eldest son of John (son of Robert Carver), was born 1658, died at Marshfield, Mass., 1760 age 102, and is noticed by Gov. Hutchinson and Dr. Belknap in the biography of Gov. Carver as the grandson of the Governor; but in Pemberton's MS. Journal, in the library of the Massachusetts Historical Society, he is called "the nephew of Governor Carver, being his brother's son."

John Carver, the father of William, died 1679 age 42, leaving a widow, Millicent, who was daughter of William Ford, and eight children. He was the son of Robert Carver, one of the founders of Marshfield, Mass., and brothers of Governor John Carver of Plymouth Colony.

Mrs. Haxton, in her Mayflower Descendants refers to "the obnoxious claims of the other Carvers to the relationship with Governor John Carver of Plymouth." She evidently was not familiar with the Pemberton Manuscripts which establishes the relationship of the "other Carvers" beyond question.

The armorial bearings of the Carver family indicate that it was one of great antiquity, and that some members of it took part in the Holy War. These are described as

Arms—Argent on a chevron a fleur-de-lis, or.

Crest—Out of a ducal coronet, or, a Saracen's head couped at the shoulders proper.

Thomas Standish, by his wife, Mary (Carver) Standish, had issue:

David Standish (see record).

Amos.

Thomas.

Mary.

William.

Betty.

David Standish, eldest son of Thomas and Mary (Carver) Standish, was born in Marshfield, Mass., 1725. The family Bible states that he "dyed June the 4th, Thursday, 4 o'clock, the 70th year of his adge, 1795." His wife "dyed Tuesday eve, 9 o'clock, 75 years of her age, Aug. ye 23, anno. 1803." Either this David or his son, David, belonged to a company of militia under the command of Capt. Thomas Turner, which marched, April 20, 1775, in response to the "alarm from Lexington; and again in the same company, as a part of Col. Theophilus Cotton's regiment, marched to R. I. agreeably to resolve of the General Court of Mass., Sep. 25, 1777." He or his son, David, was a member of Capt. William Wosten's company, raised to serve on the Gurnell, for the harbor of Plymouth, July to Oct., 1770.

David Standish married Hannah Magoun, and had issue:

Lemon.

Olivia Standish (see record).

Olivia Standish, daughter of David and Hannah (Magoun) Standish, was born May 29, 1748; married to Stockbridge Josselyn.

Stockbridge Josselyn, by his wife, Olivia (Standish) Josselyn, had issue:

I. *Olivia Josselyn*, born Nov. 10, 1769; married to Hon. William Brown Slocum (see record).

II. Stockbridge, born Feb. 25, 1772.

III. Abigail, born June 23, 1774.

IV. Lucy, born April 9, 1777; died unmarried.

V. Ruth, born April 1, 1779; married to Capt. Daniel Hall.

VI. Seth, born Dec. 5, 1782.

VII. James, born Nov. 13, 1785.

VIII. Christopher, born May 2, 1788.

IX. Amasa, born Feb. 24, 1790.

Olivia Josselyn, eldest child of Stockbridge Josselyn and his wife, Olivia (Standish) Josselyn, was married to Hon. William Brown Slocum, April 28, 1793.

Hon. William Brown Slocum, by his wife, Olivia (Josselyn) had issue, nine children, all born in Rensselaer County, New York:

I. Mary, born 1795; married to John H. Groesbeck. She died in Cincinnati, Ohio, Sept. 6, 1852, and was the mother of the following children:

1. Margaret Ann; married to Robert Burnet.
2. Herman; married to Rosina Benoist, in Covington, Kentucky.
3. William; " Elizabeth Burnet, in Cincinnati, Ohio.
4. Olivia; " Gen. Joseph Hooker.
5. Mary; " A. S. Sullivan.
6. Lucy; " T. G. Gaylord.
7. Augustus; died early.
8. John Brown; married to Genevieve Wilson, in Cincinnati.

II. Almira, born 1797; died in Raymertown, N. Y., unmarried. She was noted for her piety and good works.

III. Isaac.

IV. *Joseph Slocum*, born 1800 (see record).

V. Hiram, born May 2, 1802; married Elizabeth Van Vechten.

VI. Eliza; married to Augustus Strong.

VII. William Brown; died in New Orleans, La., unmarried.

VIII. Maria; married to Clark Perry, in 1831; died at Raymertown, N. Y.

IX. Lucy Josselyn, died about 1828, at Schaghticoke, N. Y.

Hon. Joseph Slocum, fourth child of Hon. William Brown Slocum and his wife, Olivia (Josselyn) Slocum, was born in Schaghticoke township, Rennselaer County, New York, in 1800. He settled in Syracuse, N. Y., where he became a successful merchant and a leader in public affairs. He was elected to the State Legislature in 1849. He subsequently made a journey to Russia, and was employed by that Government to establish agricultural schools in the Empire, and to import American improvements in agricultural implements. One of the first plows he took to that country was placed in the Russian National Museum as an object of great interest. He died in Syracuse, March 20, 1863, and was buried in Oakwood Cemetery. He lived an honored and useful life, and left a bright example of true manhood and uprightness of character; such a man never dies, "his works do follow him, and his memory is cherished by those who come after him." The local papers referred to him as "a man of large intellect, fine education and gentlemanly attainments, possessed of the most liberal views on all

Hon. Joseph Slocum

Margaret Pierson Jermain

matters. As a legislator he served with fidelity to his constituents and honor to himself." He married in Cambridge, Washington County, N. Y., May 4, 1825, Margaret Pierson Jermain, daughter of Major John Jermain, first of White Plains, Westchester County, N. Y., and later of Sag Harbor, Long Island (see record of Major John Jermain).

In a work published in 1907, entitled, "Memorials of Love," it being "A Sermon by Rev. George B. Spalding, D.D., LL.D., pastor of the first Presbyterian Church, Syracuse, N. Y., May 19, 1907, in reference to the western Transept Window, erected by Margaret Olivia Slocum Sage and Joseph Jermain Slocum, in loving memory of their father and mother, Joseph Slocum and Margaret Pierson Slocum, and the eastern Transept Window, erected by Margaret Olivia Slocum Sage, as a Memorial of the pastor of her childhood, Rev. John Watson Adams, D.D.:"

Dr. Spalding said: "Ten years ago Mrs. Russell Sage and her brother, Joseph Jermain Slocum, erected in the choir loft of the former church a window, in loving memory of their father, Joseph Slocum, and their mother, Margaret Jermain Slocum, This window, greatly enlarged, has found its fitting place in the western transept of the new edifice.

"Mr. Joseph Slocum, the father, was a charter member of the first Board of Trustees, of whom Hon. A. J. Northrop said in his fine historical address on the occasion of the Seventy-fifth Anniversary of the Church, in 1899: 'They were pioneers of Presbyterianism within the limits of old Syracuse, strong and true men, who were foremost in public affairs, and in laying the foundations of the institutions and the prosperity we thankfully enjoy;' and of the mother, Margaret Pierson Jermain, it has been said by one who carries the traditions of this churche's precious jewels in the treasury of her heart: 'An Elect Lady by birth and environment, for the law of the Lord governed the household into which she was born, and in this holy law she loved to meditate with an abiding trust in its promises, and a quick faith which never wavered, even when gathering years, with their varied experiences, brought their sorrows and perplexities. As wife and mother, she ordered well the ways of her household. As a friend, she was loyal, and much given to hospitality, and gifted with a peculiarly sweet and generous nature. Fulfilled to her was the promise, 'With long life will I satisfy thee,' for it was granted her to spend an honored old age in the homes of her daughter and son, and to see growing up around her children's children of the third and fourth generations.'

"The filial love and gratitude of the children of such parents, as expressed in this window, we, as a church, will keep sacred while these walls endure.

"And now, to-day, we receive another deposit of this daughter's tender affection, another window by which her great loving heart would perpetuate its tender esteem of her 'child's pastor,' the first minister of this church, Rev. John Watson Adams, D.D., who baptized Margaret Olivia Slocum and her brother, and received her into church membership.

"The gifted artist has caught the wonderful scene of our Lord's baptism by John, in the Jordan. Our Savior's feet stand in the flowing stream. His face is turned upward as the water from the shell in the Baptist's hands is poured upon him. The face, flooded with the light of the descending dove, the eyes suffused with deepest feeling, are the full expression of a spirit of mingled devotion, perfect submission and adoring love.

"The marvellous scene is bordered upon the sides with faces of the Apostles yet to be called, and above, in canopies of softened splendor, the faces of angels, radient in beauty, look down with blessing.

"In the name of this church, which is receiving into its keeping these treasures of art and commemorating affection, I congratulate the artist on this successful completion of months of labor and earnest prayers. In the name of this church I express its gratitude of Mrs. Sage for her continued love to this church, and for this splended memorial to its first pastor; pastor of the church's childhood as of her own. This church will cherish and preserve with loving care the new monument of affection and incentive to worship."

Thus the memory of these two bright and shining lights in the Christian world will ever be kept green, and the motto inscribed on the Slocum arms, that "virtue outlives the grave," will have a perfect fulfillment, as

"Only the actions of the just
Look green, and flourish in the dust."

The ancestral line of the mother, whose memory has thus been perpetuated, is shown in the record of Major John Jermain and that of his wife, Margaret Pierson.

Owing to the loss of many important records during the War of the Revolution the ancestral line of Major John Jermain has not been clearly established.

One account states that "The sufferings endured by the inhabitants of Westchester were not due alone to the outrages inflicted by the Royal Army, but by the Commissioned Officers of the American Army who had been sent into the country for the protection of the inhabitants and of their properties. The Committee of Safety addressed a letter to the President of the Continental Congress, stating that the Court House and the remains of the village at the White Plains, which had been spared on

Huguenot Memorial Window

Presented to the New York Historical Society by Mrs. Russell Sage

One of the most beautiful works of art, as well as of historic interest that adorns the new building of the New York Historical Society, is the Memorial Window presented to the Society by Mrs. Russell Sage in recognition of the little colony of Huguenots, who, forced by continued persecutions on account of their religion, fled from their homes in France, and sought refuge in Holland, England and Scotland, and finally found a safe asylum in the Province of New York. Of this little colony was one of the ancestors of Mrs. Russell Sage. This Memorial will be appreciated by the descendants of the little colony of Huguenots who founded and named the town of New Rochelle in Westchester County, N. Y., and affords cause for congratulation that the memory of their ancestors is thus to be perpetuated. This is also intended as a memorial to Mrs. Martha J. Lamb, the well known historian and founder of the Huguenot Society.

This beautiful Memorial Window is the work of Miss Mary Tillinghast, a famous New York artist, who is also a descendant of the Huguenot refugees. The work has been much admired and favorably noticed by the art critics of the New York press.

The subject is "The Revocation of the Edict of Nantes."

The scene in the main openings shows a room at Fontainbleau with a view of the park through the long windows where, according to tradition, Louis XIV signed the Revocation.

The King, Louis XIV, is shown in a costume of tones of white, richly embroidered, and robed in a mantle of royal purple bordered with ermine, and wearing the tall perruque and the high heels he affected to increase his height. He is surrounded by attendant courtiers robed in the rich costumes of the period. At the King's feet kneels a soldier clad in armour, helmet in hand, receiving the royal command to fight the enemies of the Church. The pose of Louis is vigorous and imposing, as he points with his sword to the Imperial Decree bearing the words "La Revocation de l'Edit de Nantes."

The regal figure of Madame de Maintenon appears in the opening at the right, beautifully arrayed in court costume of white and gold brocade, with a long train of rose satin which she is holding back, with one hand, in a pose of exceptional beauty and dignity.

The architectural features carry out the general scheme of the room at Fontainbleau.

The coat of arms in the upper part of the left opening is that of Henry of Navarre, and is surmounted by his medallion portrait.

In the upper part of the opening is the coat of arms of James II, who succored the Huguenots in their distress. Above it appears a medallion of Louis XIV, after the Revocation Medal struck at Rome in commemoration of the Edict of Nantes.

"The Huguenot Lovers" (after Millais) are shown in the medallion over the centre opening.

The following inscription is placed in the base of the window: "In commemoration of the Huguenots who fled to America owing to the Revocation of the Privileges according by the Edict of Nantes,"

February, 1599. October, 1685.

the retreat of our forces, was, after the enemy had in their turn retired, wantonly destroyed without the Order, and to the infinite regret of our worthy General. In addition to the destruction of the Court House, with all its valuable records, the church was burned on the night of the 5th of November, 1776. Thus the town and church records were entirely destroyed, and many of the inhabitants fled after their houses and other property was destroyed by the so-called "patriots."

It is a well known fact that in the little Huguenot family settled at New Rochelle there was a family of Jermains. The name is found in the marriage records of New York City and in several towns on Long Island. The State rosters and Revolutionary Rolls contains some of this name who served in the patriot army.

Among the numerous French families that fled to England and Scotland after the Revocation of the Edict of Nantes were the Jermains, or Jermyns, as the name is frequently spelled, and some of the descendants fled to America during the latter part of the seventeenth and early part of the eighteenth centuries.

In the absence of all documentary evidence concerning the direct ancestral of Major John Jermain, his descendants may point with pride to him as the founder of the family in this country. Not a single "black sheep" has ever been found among them, and the family escutcheon remains untarnished. The public and private life of Major John Jermain and the splendid record of his descendants show that he must come of an excellent family, endowed with great intellectual and moral attainments.

It has always been claimed, with many facts to substantiate such claim, that Major John Jermain was a descendant of one of the numerous families of Huguenots who fled to this country from France and England. Baird's "Huguenot Emigration to America," vol. ii., page 268, says: "Jean Germin, or Germaine, was a native of Trimblade, in the province of Saintange."

"Jean Germin, fugitif de la Trimblade. He was one of the Narragansett (R. I.) settlers in 1686.

"During the Indian hostilities in Rhode Island many of the Huguenot families who had settled there were obliged to flee for their lives.

"Upon leaving Narragansett, the refugees became widely scattered. Among those who left and joined other settlements were the Germaines, and the name appears on the records in different parts of the State of New York and on Long Island. It is spelled Germin, Germaine, Jermyn and Jermaine. The same is spelled in a variety of ways in England, Scotland and Wales. Jean Germaine is John Germaine, or Jermaine, in English; the pronunciation is almost identical in the original."

Major John Jermain was born in Westchester County, New York, May 20, 1758. That his educational opportunities were favorable to the development of his intellectual inheritance is shown in his subsequent business and public career. There can be no question of his patriotism, and of his ardent devotion to the cause of American Independence. If he was not on the "fighting line" in the front ranks of the patriot army, he was certainly in the line of duty from the beginning to the close of the war, and he determined to perpetuate that event so far as lay in his power by naming his youngest son after the Father of his Country. The Revolutionary Rolls of the State of New York are very incomplete, and even within the past few years muster rolls were found in obscure corners of the State Archives, where they had remained since the close of the war, and it will not be at all surprising if additional lists are discovered, showing the names and record of many who rendered important service in defence of their country. Probably at the close of the war he moved to Long Island, where he married Margaret Pierson, and from that time forward his life was an open book, "to be seen and read of all men."

The date of his removal to Sag Harbor (in the town of Southampton), Long Island, is not definitely known; but he engaged in business there, and was no doubt successful in his several undertakings, as he accumulated considerable property for those days. The Southampton Town Records contain the following, vol. iii., page 338-9: "Whereas, the Trustees of Southampton, on the third day of December, in the year 1782, did grant unto Nathan Fordham, and Ebenezer White, Esq., and Deacon David Hodges, the pond called Otter pond, lying near Sagg Harbour, with all the privileges of said Pond, and likewise the privileges to dig across the road to have said pond to communicate with the salt water as ordered; to make a Fish Pond, together with the privileges of the brook that may run from said pond, so that the fish may not be hindered from coming in; to them, their heirs, and assigns forever, provided always that they do and shall well and truly make and maintain a good and sufficient bridge across said brook, at least twelve feet wide, with a rail on each side of the same, suitable for all sorts of carriages to pass over on; and Whereas, the proprietors of said pond did, on the eighteenth day of February, in the year one thousand seven hundred and ninety-three, petition to the trustees that the above-said grant, with the privileges of the pond, should be transferred to John Jermain, with the privilege to set mills on the stream. Voted that the above-said grant for the Otter Pond, together with the privileges belonging to the same, with liberty to put mills on the stream, be transferred to John Jermain, his heirs and assigns forever; provided always that he do and shall well and truly make and maintain a good and sufficient bridge over said brook,

Major John Jermain

The Old Jermain Homestead at Sag Harbor, Long Island

seventeen feet wide, with a road on each side of the same, and boarded up to said rail, suitable for all sorts of carriages to pass over; and further, that the said John Jermain have liberty to dig across the road in order to let the water of Crooked Pond and Little Long Pond into said pond; provided always that he do and shall well and truly make and maintain good and sufficient bridges across said brooks for all sorts of carriages to pass.

Henry Corwither, Jonathan Roger,
John Fordham, Rufus Foster,
David Hodges, Daniel Howell,
Uriah Rogers, James White,
David Hains, Jeremiah Post,
David Hulsey.

Per Caleb Cooper, Clerk.

A true copy, compared and examined by me,

Wm. Herrick, Clerk."

Major John Jermain was an enterprising, public-spirited citizen, and entered heartily into every project for the improvement and development of his adopted town. He was a model husband, a tender and affectionate father, and an upright, honorable citizen, who enjoyed to the fullest extent the confidence and esteem of his neighbors, as well as that of his fellow citizens, throughout Suffolk County. He died at Sag Harbor, Long Island, February 17, 1819, leaving a will, of which the following is a certified copy:

WILL OF MAJOR JOHN JERMAIN, OF SOUTHAMPTON, LONG ISLAND.

In the name of God, Amen. I, John Jermain, of the Town of Southampton, in the County of Suffolk and State of New York, Merchant, being of sound mind and memory, thanks be given unto God for the same, therefore, calling unto mind the mortality of my body, and knowing that is appointed for all men once to die, do make and ordain this my last will and testament, that is to say: First, I give my soul to God, with a hope of salvation threw the merits of Jesus Christ our Lord, and with regard to my worldly estate, after paying my just debts, and allowing my wife her Dower, it is my will that a distribution of my Estate be made to Silvanus Jermain, Rebecca Spooner, Juleaan Prime, Alanson Jermain, Caroline Jermain, John Jermain, Jun., George W. Jermain, and Margaret Jermain the 2nd, or the younger, to their heirs and assigns forever.

But as my children are all dear and dutiful to me alike, I wish a just distribution of my property to each of them; therefore, it is necessary here to mention that Rebecca

Spooner and Juleaan Prime has been advanced out of my estate for thare furnature, beding, and out fits to the ampt of three hundred dollars each, and Sylvanus P. Jermain and Alanson Jermain for their education and other expenses have had, I should say two hundred dollars more than John and George; and it is my will that this may be adjusted equal and in brotherly love, also the amount that was advanced out of my estate to my dear departed daughter, Poley. I wish that to be given to her three children, Elbert Daniel, Jun., and Mary Latham, at the discretion of their Father, Daniel Latham, and my wife, Margaret Jermain; and,

Lastly, I constitute and appoint my beloved wife, Margaret Jermain, Silvanus P. Jermain, and Alanson Jermain, executors of this my last will and testament.

In witness whereof, I have hereunto set my hand and seal this seventh day of June, in the year of our Lord, one thousand eight hundred and eleven.

Signed, sealed and declared by the said John Jermain, to be his last will and testament, in presents of each of us the subscribers witness:

Abraham Corey,
Wm. Ramond,
Charles Douglass.

John Jermain (L. S.)

Proved March 23, 1819.

Recorded in Suffolk County Surrogate Office, in Liber. D. of Wills, at page 191.

State of New York,
Suffolk County, Surrogate's Court.

I, Robert W. Duvall, Clerk of the Surrogate's Court of the said County, do hereby certify that I have compared the foregoing copy of the will of John Jermain, deceased, with the original record thereof, now remaining in this office, and have found the same to be a correct transcript therefrom, and of the whole of the said original record.

In Witness Whereof, I have hereunto set my hand and affixed the seal of office, the 10th day of February, in the year of our Lord, one thousand nine hundred and eight.

Robert W. Duvall,
Clerk of the Surrogate's Court.

Major Jermain is said to have served in the Westchester Militia during the War of the Revolution. He commanded the fort at Sag Harbor in the War of 1812-15; and this was one of the most exposed points on the Long Island coast, a large fleet of British ships being almost constantly stationed near the entrance to New London harbor, and cruising around near the mouth of the Connecticut river, watching for American privateers, which were constantly engaged in preying on British commerce.

Unfortunately, all the records pertaining to the defence of Long Island during the War of 1812, except the town of Brooklyn, have been lost. That Major Jermain saw active service during that period there can be no doubt. His title of "Major" was honestly earned, and was by no means a merely "ornamental" one.

Major John Jermain married, August 27, 1781, Margaret, daughter of Sylvanus Pierson, of Bridgehampton, L. I., son of Josiah, son of Colonel Henry, son of Henry Pierson, founder of the Long Island branch of the Pierson family, and brother of Rev. Abraham Pierson (see Pierson family).

THE PIERSON FAMILY OF ENGLAND AND AMERICA

In the various accounts published of Rev. Abraham Pierson, of Connecticut, and Henry Pierson, of Southampton, Long Island, no attempt has been made to establish the relationship between them. The marriage records of England, however, have established the fact beyond question that they were brothers, and came of a family of considerable distinction, having been honored by their sovereign for distinguished services rendered, as shown by their armorial bearings, which are nearly the same as those borne by the Dean of Salisbury, viz.:

Pierson

Arms—Three suns in pale, or, between two palets erminois.

Crest—A demi lion proper, holding in the dexter paw a sun or.

Motto—Mea spes est in Deo (My hope is in God).

From the English Church Records:

I. Richard Pierson, of St. Mary's, Aldermeary, married, 1540, Elizabeth, daughter of Edward Church, by Thomassine, daughter of Liman Hendon. Children:

1. Henry, married Anne —— [She married, 2ndly, Oct. 25, 1567, Thomas Chamberlaine.]
    1. Anne, Aug. 10, 1586, married Thomas L. Wilbraham.
2. Edward.
3. Richard Pierson (see record).
4. Margaret.

II. Richard Pierson, Jr., son of above-named Richard, of St. Mary, Aldermeary, born 1545; married, July 1, 1567, Johann Harwood. Issue:

1. Henry Pierson.

III. Henry Pierson, son of Richard Pierson, Jr., of St. Mary, Aldermeary, born 1568; married ——. He was the father of

IV. Abraham Pierson, of Shadwell, Parish of Stepney, Middlesex, born 1590; married, July 31, 1615, Christian Johnson, widow, and had

1. Abraham, born 1616; Trinity College, Cambridge, 1632; A.M., 1636; came to New England 1639, first to Lynn, Mass.; Southampton, Long Island, 1640-1647; Branford, Conn., 1647-66; Newark, N. J., 1666, to his death.

Henry Pierson, son of Abraham (1) and Christian (Johnson) Pierson, was born in England, 1618; came to New England with his brother, Rev. Abraham. He settled first at Lynn, Mass., and removed thence, with his brother and a small colony, from Lynn to Southampton, Long Island. [The place was named from Southampton, England; called by the Indians *"Ag-wam,"* a place abounding in fish.]

Henry Pierson, like his brother, was a man of deep piety and strong religious convictions, as well as fine scholarly attainments, and a leader in public affairs of the town. Both he and his brother labored earnestly for the temporal and spiritual upbuilding of the town, until the latter removed to Branford, in 1647. From that time forward Henry was the leading spirit of the town, notably in educational matters, and is said to have been the founder of the common school system of America.

The town of Southampton was incorporated by patent, under Governor Andros, Nov. 1, 1676, confirmed by Governor Dongan, Dec. 6, 1686, and recognized as a town March 7, 1788. The Trustees named in the first patent were: John Topping, John Howell, Thomas Halsey, Sen., Jos. Raynor, Edward Howell, John Jagger, John Foster, Francis Sayre, Jos. Fordham, *Henry Pierson,* John Cooper (father-in-law of Henry Pierson), Ellis Cook, Samuel Clarke, Rich. Post, and John Jennins.

Henry Pierson was elected Clerk of Suffolk County, L. I., in 1669, and held that position till 1681. He wrote a clear, bold, scholarly hand, a rare accomplishment in those days. He was consulted on all matters relating to transfers, judicial and local government affairs. A deed signed by Nathaniel Pierson, one of his descendants, is written in a clear, bold, beautiful hand, an evidence of family inheritance. Most of Henry's descendants were men of culture and scholarly attainments. Henry Pierson married Mary, daughter of John Cooper.

John Cooper, of Lynn, Mass., came from England in the Hopewell, in 1635, aged 41, with his wife Wibroe and children, Mary aged 13, John 10, Thomas 7, and Martha 5. He was a son of Edward Cooper. He came to Southampton with the colony from Lynn, and was one of the Trustees named in the original patent under Governor Andros.

Henry Pierson (1) by his wife Mary (Cooper) Pierson had issue

Abigail, born 1649.
Joseph, " 1656.
Henry Pierson (2)—see record below.
Benjamin, moved to New Jersey.
Theodore, born 1669.
Sarah, " January 20, 16—.

Col. Henry Pierson, third child of Henry (1) and Mary (Cooper) Pierson, was born at Southampton, 1652. He was a man of superior education, cultured and refined in manners, and a gentleman in the highest sense of the term; prominent in military affairs, a thorough organizer and strict desciplinarian. He was elected to the General Assembly of the Province of New York and was reelected for several successive terms, together with his brother-in-law, Col. Matthew Howell. He served on all the important committees and did much in shaping legislation and laying the foundations of of our Colonial and State laws. He was Speaker of the Assembly from 1690 to 1695, and was associated with the leading statesmen and other public men of that period. He deserves to rank high among the great founders of the Empire State. He married Susanna, daughter of Major John Howell, son of Edward.

Edward Howell came with his family to Boston in 1639, and was admitted freeman of the Massachusetts Bay Colony in March of the same year. He soon removed to Lynn, where he had a grant of 500 acres. During the winter of 1639-40 a new settlement was proposed on Long Island of which he seems to have been the leader, as the compact, or agreement of terms of founding the plantation is in his handwriting, as well as the laws adopted by the first settlers, and to the last year of his life he was always Magistrate and a member of the General Court at Hartford, Conn., Southampton then being under the jurisdiction of Connecticut.

The Howells sprang from a Knightly family who descend from one of the ancient families of North Wales. The armorial bearings are recorded in the College of Heraldry, described as

Arms.—Three towers, triple-towered, argent.

Crest.—Out of a ducal coronet or, a rose argent, stalked and leaved vert, between two wings endorsed of the last.

Edward Howell, by his wife Frances, had six children, of whom John was the third.

Major John Howell, son of Edward and Frances Howell, was baptized Nov. 22, 1624. He was a man of distinction, and one who, more than any other of his contemporaries in Southampton was entrusted with the management of public business, especially in its greater relations with New England and the colonial government of New York. By his wife Susannah, he had eleven children of whom Susanna was the sixth.

Col. Henry Pierson, by his wife Susannah (Howell) Pierson, had issue eight children, viz :

1. John, born Nov. 30, 1685.
2. David, born 1688.
3. Hannah,
4. Sarah.
5. Theophilus, born 1690.
6. Abraham, " 1693.
7. Josiah Pierson, born 1695. (See record).
8. Mary.

Josiah Pierson seventh child of Col. Henry by his wife Mary (Howell) Pierson, was born 1695. He lived the life of a quiet industrious farmer with no ambition for public or military affairs. He was four times married, and raised a large family of children, many of whom lived honorable lives and perpetuated the virtues of the Pierson Family. Of these there were

I. Silas.
II. Matthew, born 1725.
III. Sylvanus Pierson, born 1727. (See record).
IV. Paul.
V. Timothy.
VI. Josiah.
VII. Joseph.
VIII. Benjamin.
IX. John.
X. Martha, married to Stephen Jagger.
XI. Susannah, married to David Hodges.

Sylvanus Pierson, third child of Josiah Pierson, was born March 2, 1725; died at

Bridgehampton, L. I., Aug. 23, 1795. He married Rebecca Lupton, daughter of David Lupton, of Boston, Mass. Their children were

I. Rebecca.

II. Margaret.

III. Sally.

IV. Margaret Pierson, married to John Jermain.

The children of Major John Jermain and his wife Margaret (Pierson) Jermain were

I. Mary, born May 7, 1782; died at Sag Harbor, Long Island, Jan. 28, 1811. She was married to Daniel Latham at Sag Harbor, Feb. 19th, 1800. He died at Sag Harbor, Nov. 15, 1830.

II. Silvanus Pierson Jermain, born Jan. 31, 1784; died at Albany, N. Y., April 20, 1869. He married Catharine Barclay, at Albany, N. Y., Aug. 1, 1807. She died at Albany, N. Y., Jan. 24 1816.

III. Rebecca, born Oct. 2, 1787; died in Brooklyn, N, Y., Nov. 15, 1824. She was married to Col. Alden Spooner, Feb. 24, 1807. He died in Brooklyn, N. Y., Nov. 24, 1848.

IV. Julie Ann, born Jan. 31, 1789; died at White Plains, N. Y., Aug. 24, 1874. She was married to Rev. Nathaniel Scudder Prime, D.D., at Sag Horbor, L. I., July 5, 1808. He died at Mamaroneck, N. Y., March 27, 1856.

V. Alanson, born Feb. 10, 1791; died Nov. 5, 1885; married Sabra Rice at Albany, N. Y., Jan. 12, 1820. She died in New York City, May 13, 1841.

VI. Caroline, born Jan. 25, 1794; married Rev. Stephen Porter, at Sag Harbor, L. I., June 9, 1812; died at Geneva, N. Y., June 18, 1877.

VII. John, born March 22, 1796; died at Detroit, Mich., March 15, 1881. He married, at Ovid, N. Y., April 13, 1820, Sarah Delavan; she died Jan, 14, 1890.

VIII. George Washington, born Sept. 29, 1798; died at Geneva, N. Y., Sept. 21, 1879. He married Cornelia Wendell, Jan. 13, 1820; she died at Lockport, N. Y., Sept. 6, 1857; he married 2ndly, Jan. 9, 1859, Abigail P. Warner, at Milwaukee, Wis.

IX. *Margaret Pierson Jermain,* born March 4, 1804. (See record below).

Margaret Pierson Jermain, youngest child of Major John Jermain and his wife Margaret (Pierson) Jermain, was born March 4, 1804. She died at Cedarhurst, Long

Island, at the home of her daughter, Mrs. Russell Sage, July 19, 1891. She was a woman of fine intellectual gifts, a devout, and concientious Christian, with great firmness of character; at the same time, a gentle loving mother, and the highest type of true womanhood. She was greatly beloved in the community where she resided during her married life, which was devoted to deeds of charity and love. She was married, at Cambridge, N. Y., May 4, 1825, to Joseph Slocum.

The children of Hon. Joseph Slocum and his wife Margaret Pierson (Jermain) Slocum were:

Margaret Olivia Slocum (see record below); married Nov. 24, 1869, at Albany, N. Y., to Hon. Russell Sage.

Joseph Jermain Slocum, born June 24, 1833.

Margaret Olivia (Slocum) Sage, eldest child of Hon. Joseph Slocum and his wife, Margaret Pierson (Jermain), was born at Syracuse, N. Y. She inherits, without doubt, the best traits of her distinguished ancestors whose personal history has already been given. Environment has been favorable to the development of these characteristics. Only those who had enjoyed the most intimate acquaintance with her could appreciate the qualities of mind and heart, and the noble qualities with which nature has endowed her. This delightful task was undertaken by a classmate and one of her closest friends, who, after referring to her ancestral line says:

"From such a parentage it follows that Margaret Olivia Slocum was blessed with rare mental endowments and a harmony of character that have signally qualified her for an active and conspiciously useful career.

"She enjoyed in childhood and early youth the advantages of the best private schools of Syracuse, always loving study for its own sake, and readily mastering the elementary branches, so that at twelve years of age she found pleasure in rhetoric and pastime in the brilliant marvels of astronomy.

"Through happy childhood she grew as a flower reaches to the light, full of ecstacy of existence, but with a tender concientiousness that foreshadowed an earnest womanhood. She was but a child in years when she wrote in her dairy as the motto of her life:

"Count that day lost, whose low descending sun
Views from thy hand no worthy actions done.

"In 1846 she entered Troy Seminary and graduated in 1847.

"The following year was passed in her home in Syracuse, until through the financial reverses of her father she resolved to become a teacher. In furtherance of this purpose she secured a position with her friend and former teacher in Troy, Miss Harriette

Dilaye, who, with Miss Mary L. Bonney, was then at the head of Chestnut Street Seminary of Philadelphia, since become renowned as Ogontz School.

"There Miss Slocum remained for two years, meeting her responsibilities with cheerful efficiency until her overtaxed strength required a respite.

"Later she resumed teaching for a while, but from impaired health, only at brief intervals. In 1869 she became the second wife of Hon. Russell Sage, the well known financier of New York City, and whom she had known from childhood.

"Amid the responsibilities of her social position, through the years of her married and affluent life, she has been true to her early motto.

"Her benefactions have been unstinted, and her executive ability in her public philanthropies has already passed into history. Officially connected with the Women's Christian Union as Treasurer, the Woman's Hospital for thirty years, the Woman's Exchange, Home and Foreign Missions, besides other local organizations, she has for many years served the interests of these institutions with conspicuous fidelity.

"Mrs. Sage has been President of the Emma Willard Association from its beginning in 1891 for which office her fine presence and recognized administrative qualities eminently fit her.

"She is zealously devoted to the aims of the organizations in the furtherance of which she has been liberally aided by her husband. In 1894, Mrs. Sage was chosen by the Board of Trustees of the Emma Willard School, (successor to Troy Seminary) to act with them.

"Of the seventeen trustees, four may be women, and Mrs. Sage was awarded the honor of being the first to serve in that capacity with the honorable body. To her zealous efforts in behalf of the future of this historic school, perpetuating the name and fame of Emma Willard, and the cordial sympathy and co-operation of her husband in his far-reaching plans, we owe the revival of interest in this famous institution, and the new departure that has for its object the fullest equipment for the high and liberal education of women.

"On the occasion of the first commencement exercises of the Emma Willard School, in 1897, Mrs. Sage was the recipient of a valuable testimonial from the Emma Willard Association—a beautiful pin, the design of which is a gold scroll, with a coronet of four large diamonds at the top, an enameled bow-knot underneath in imitation of the pink ribbon emblem of the school. The monogram 'E. W. A.' is encrusted with diamonds.

"Heartily in touch with the progress of events, Mrs. Sage, in her deductions and opinions, gives evidence of a comprehensive mind and a generous judgment. She is a fine conversationalist, abundant in anecdote and amiable in repartee. In the cultivated society of New York she is known as a genial hostess, who gracefully sustains the dignity of her prominent position without ostentation. She is a member of the Collegiate Church of St. Nicholas, 48th Street and Fifth Avenue, New York City, and attends the First Presbyterian Church at Far Rockaway, Long Island, near her country home at Cedarhurst, L. I."

After the death of her husband, Mrs. Sage was called upon to assume the responsibility of managing the immense estate left to her discretion as executrix, and, with the exception of a few bequests, the chief beneficiary under the will. So great was the confidence of Mr. Sage in her ability to handle and dispose of his accumulated millions, that there was not a single qualification or restriction specified in the will.

With the wisdom of a Solomon, with the mature judgment of a Judge in Equity, and with a generosity that does credit to her heart as well as her business sagacity, she has met and overcome the serious difficulties that beset her pathway. Litigations were threatened on every side from near and distant relatives. These were met in the same generous spirit that has characterized every act of her life, and a satisfactory compromise was effected. In her own benefactions she has chosen wisely, and given where, in her opinion, the result of long experience, the greatest good could be accomplished; and it goes without saying that in the future "thousands will rise up to call her blessed." In dealing with the old employees of her husband, who had served him faithfully for many years, she generously doubled the amount of their salaries. No woman ever experienced in a greater degree the scriptural assurance that "it is more blessed to give than to receive." Her whole life has been spent in doing good and contributing to the happiness of others.

Those who have known Mrs. Sage only as the gentle, sympathetic, Christian woman, could realize that she is also a woman of indomnitable will, fearless and self-possessed, and equal to any emergency. Incidents in her life, known only to a few of her most intimate friends, have proved this beyond question. In this respect she is one woman among a thousand.

To enumerate all her great educational, charitable and other noble enterprises, would be simply a repetition that would add but little to her reputation as one of the greatest philanthropists and public benefactors of the present age. The greatest of all these is her gift to the Emma Willard School, of Troy.

The Troy *Press*, in its issue of April 4, 1908, referring to Mrs. Russell Sage's gift to the Emma Willard School of that city, said, editorially:

"The broadside of beautiful buildings projected by the Emma Willard School, presented to-day, and made possible by the munificence of Mrs. Russell Sage, the most eminent graduate from this venerable, victorious and renowned institution, will be viewed with pleasure and pride by our people. This presentation is representative of an epochal change in the direction of development, and prophetic of an ampler magnitude, which will assure the attainment of a collegiate classification in the near future. Incidentally this School will play its full part in making Troy one of the leading educational centres of the country—a very valuable moral and material asset for any community. The R. P. I., in a different way, will perform a similar function. Factors such as these contribute to the culture and civilization of society. The cause of humanity is under heavy obligations to noble women of the type of Emma Willard and Mrs. Russell Sage, whose names will be inseparably interlinked in the progressive history of the Emma Willard School."

In a supplement of the same date, containing illustrations of the buildings, the same paper says:

"The magnificent group of buildings depicted in to-day's supplement is reproduced from the plans for the new Emma Willard School, to be erected on the site on Pawling Avenue, purchased by the trustees of that institution with a portion of the $1,000,000 given her Alma Mater by Mrs. Russell Sage. In architectural beauty, completeness of equipment and ideality of location, these superb scholastic structures, when finished, will be second to none in the country. They will enable the school to extend its work in all departments to the highest standard of efficiency, and do for the cause of higher education for women, with Troy as a centre, more than any act in recent years.

"The new location of the splendid old school is one of the most sightly in this section, and in that respect, also, the institution will occupy a commanding position. The new buildings will stand on a tract of about thirty acres, much of which will be utilized immediately, while eventually every inch of it will be devoted to some useful purpose. The buildings will face Pawling Avenue, with Elm Grove Avenue on the side.

"Introductorily, it is fitting to point out that one of the results of the generous gift of Mrs. Sage is to move the school from a congested city block, which half a century ago had an entirely different environment, and place it, imbued with new life and a wealth of enthusiasm, on one of the most ideal suburban sites to be afforded in any section of the State. The elevation of the tract on which the new buildings will stand varies from 320 to 400 feet above sea level. The main structures are to be placed on the crown of the hill, the ridge of which overlooks Pawling Avenue. The first floor of the residence hall will be 392, and the school hall 393 feet above the level of the

RESIDENCE HALL

An Ideal Home for the Students

sea. The trustees, with whom originated the plan to transplant the institution, contend that when the old is placed in comparison with the new site, and it is realized that the present location is not more than ten feet above the sea level, there can be no one of judgment who will not realize and appreciate the immense value of the marked change.

"The plans show a collection of buildings of such beauty in design, and so peculiarly adapted for educational purposes, that in themselves they disclose the immense amount of work entailed in their preparation by the architects to whom they are accredited. They were drawn by M. F. Cummings & Son.

"The main structures fronting on Pawling Avenue consist of a School Hall and a Residence Hall, separated by an open space, which gives an approach to the campus, the only communication between these two blocks being a cloistered passage. The Gymnasium Hall will be placed on the further side of the campus.

"The buildings known as Sage Hall, the Plum Art Museum and Gurley Memorial, are ultimately to be located around the campus. The new collection of buildings will be approached by a driveway from Pawling Avenue that will encircle the entire group, and lead the visitor to the porte-cochere, the main entrance to the Residence Hall.

"*The Residence Hall* is the most important building of the group. It will occupy the northwest corner of the campus, with a fore court overlooking Pawling Avenue. The building is three stories in height, and dominated by a tower 110 feet high. The top of the parapet of this tower will be 492 feet above sea level, and it will form one of the most prominent and lofty landmarks in this section of the State. The tower is intended to give a large water storage, which of itself will be a source of protection against fire for all the buildings. It will also be utilized to carry up the chimney flue from the power station. The lower floor of the tower will be used as a reading room. The four floors above will be devoted to studies and dormitories.

"The first floor contains a reception parlor adjoining the entrance from the porte-cochere, with the principal's, teachers', guests' writing and spare rooms located on either side of a main corridor eleven feet wide. The main staircase hall is at the further end of this trunk corridor, placed directly at the intersection of the four arms, and will be modeled on the lines of the old English hall, with a richly molded oaken staircase leading to the balconies, which gives access to the upper floors. To the west is the living room, an unusually fine apartment, 52 by 36 feet, with two large oriel bays and an inglenook fireplace recess in addition. This living room will be paneled eight feet high in oak, with beam ceilings, reminding one of the English

SCHOOL HALL

Showing Gymnasium on the left

sixteenth century living halls. East of the stair hall is the dining room, 32 by 62 feet, with large bays and fine recess in addition, with a private dining room for guests adjoining, 21 by 16 feet in dimensions. The dining room will be paneled with oak, and the ceiling will be treated after the manner of Elizabethian times. The kitchen wing communicates directly with the dining room and main corridor, comprising the housekeeper's office and rooms, serving room, kitchen 33 by 30 feet, servants' dining hall, pastry, and other rooms adjoining. The two upper stories of the kitchen wing provide for a servants' parlor and bedrooms, and are entirely separated from the rest of the block. The students have their own entrance from the corner of the fore court, with the entrance hall leading into the main stair hall. It also has an approach to the campus.

"The uppermost floor of the residence hall contains an infirmary, with every facility for the best treatment of students in case of sickness.

"The basement of the hall on the north side overlooks Elm Grove Avenue, provides for a laundry, ironing and sorting rooms, drying rooms, kitchen stores and cold stores, and communicates by elevator with the main dormitories. A sub-basement permits direct access from a kitchen yard entering from Elm Grove Avenue, making it possible for all supplies to be brought to the service wing direct, thereby avoiding the necessity for tradespeople entering the main grounds at all. It allows all refuse to be taken direct to the power station for consumption beneath the boilers.

"*The School Hall.*—This occupies the southwestern portion of the Pawling Avenue front. The students' entrance is on the north side of the fore court, with an imposing staircase hall, two stories in height, with marble balustrading and painted walls. The first floor is occupied by four primary rooms to the west, four intermediate students' rooms overlooking the campus, principal's office, secretary's office, the teachers' rooms looking on to the fore court, and is also approached from the general entrance and rotunda.

"The Library will be an exceptionally fine apartment, open to the roof, thirty-two feet wide and seventy feet long, with very fine oriels at each end and a fireplace in the centre. This library room is specially well designed for its purposes, with its open timber, hammer beam, arcaded and traceried side windows and oriels, and cannot fail to remind travelers of similar rooms in the Old World colleges, of which it is really a replica. The fireplace is especially intended as a memorial to the donor. The campus is easily accessible.

"*Assembly Room.*—This is a large room, fifty-five by forty-two feet, and is entered from the main stair hall, and will serve for the time being as a place for morning devotions. In the distant future it is hoped to furnish a fitting building on the south side of the campus, providing a chapel and general assembly hall. This Assembly Hall will be a fine apartment, with open timbered, traceried roof, tall, traceried side windows, and high paneled wood dado. The second floor of this school block is to be occupied by the academic students. It has rooms devoted to French, German, history, classics, mathematics and English, with the requisite teachers' rooms, toilets and other accessories, and a study hall fifty-three by thirty-nine feet, occupying the west front, with paneled walls and ornamental beam ceiling.

"In the basement of the school hall will be located the chemical laboratories and a large lunch hall for the students.

"*Gymnasium Hall.*—This building occupies a site on the east side of the campus, with a tower entrance. In the upper portion of the tower will be a clock, the three faces of which will be seen from any portion of the campus, and in fact also from some parts of the Pawling Avenue fore court. The main floor contains a gymnasium forty-four feet wide and ninety feet in length, lighted by large oriels, and having an oaken timber roof. The walls are fitted for the reception of gymnastic apparatus. A running track gallery is provided overhead. Fencing room, social room, office and retiring room are also on this floor, with a large piazza, from which spectators can watch the progress of the games on the athletic field to the rear. Rooms for special apparatus are on the upper floor. On the lower floor are a swimming bath, sixty-three by twenty feet, a double bowling alley, three hundred lockers, shower baths, drying rooms and toilets. A spiral stairway leads to the floor above, in addition to a main stair.

"Externally the designs provide for buildings in the English Collegiate Gothic style, such as one would expect to find in the buildings of Oxford and Cambridge, erected in the latter part of the fifteenth and during the sixteenth centuries.

"*Russell Sage Hall* is the gift of Russell Sage. This structure has five stories above the basement, and is of fireproof construction. All the floors have steel beams, with a filling of fireproof material, and all the dividing walls and partitions are of brick or hollow tiles. The building is equipped with an electric elevator, and there are two staircases, both of iron. The interior is finished in quartered oak, and the floors are of hard polished wood. The library, dining room and reception rooms are equipped with open fire-places, and the designs of the three apartments are very beautiful and artistic. Both the single and double rooms for the students are completely furnished, and the pupils need to bring only their personal belongings. Of Russell Sage Hall it may be said that it is in all the essentials a home for the students, in which the highest type of refined home life is cultivated. It is entirely separated from the other buildings, and, therefore, makes possible an atmosphere of quiet and rest.

"It was in 1907, after the death of her husband, that Mrs. Sage gave to her old school in Troy the sum of $1,000,000, and at the same time a similar amount to the Rensselaer Polytechnic Institute. Her other benefactions include $115,000 to the public school at Sag Harbor, L. I.; $350,000 to the New York Young Men's Christian Association; $150,000 to the American Seaman's Friend Society; $150,000 to the Northfield, Mass., Seminary; $300,000 to the Sage Institute of Pathology of the City Hospital on Blackwell's Island; $250,000 to a Home for Indigent Women; and $100,000 to the Syracuse University. One of Mrs. Sage's best known donations is that of $10,000,000, constituting a fund that is known as the Sage Foundation for Social Betterment."

The most interesting, as well as the most sacred, of all Mrs. Sage's gifts are the Memorial Windows to her parents, and to her old pastor in the church where, as a child, she received her baptismal name and her early religious instruction—the First Presbyterian Church of Syracuse, N. Y. A full account of these gifts is compressed in "A sermon by Rev. George B. Spalding, D.D., LL.D., Pastor of the First Presbyterian Church, Syracuse, N. Y., May 19, 1907, in reference to the Western Transept Window, erected by Margaret Olivia Slocum Sage and Joseph Jermain Slocum, in Loving Memory of their Father and Mother, Joseph Slocum and Margaret Pierson Slocum, and the Eastern Transept Window, erected by Margaret Olivia Slocum Sage, as a Memorial of the Pastor of her childhood, Rev. John Watson Adams, D.D."

Referring to these gifts Dr. Spalding said: "Ten years ago Mrs. Russell Sage and her brother, Joseph Germain Slocum, erected in the choir-loft of the former church a window in loving memory of their father, Joseph Slocum, and their mother, Margaret Germain Slocum. This window, greatly enlarged, has found its fitting place in the western transept of the new edifice.

"Mr. Slocum, the father, was a charter member of the first Board of Trustees, of whom Hon. A. J. Northrop said in his fine historical address on the occasion of the Seventy-fifth Anniversary of the Church in 1899: 'They were pioneers of Presbyterianism within the limits of old Syracuse, strong and true men, who were foremost in public affairs, and in laying the foundations of the institutions and the prosperity we thankfully enjoy;' and of the mother, Margaret Pierson Jermain, it has been said by one who carries the traditions of this church as precious jewels in the treasury of her heart: 'An Elect Lady by birth and environment, for the law of the Lord governed the household into which she was born, and in this holy law she loved to meditate, with an abiding trust in its promises, and a quick faith which never wavered even when gathering years, with their varied experiences, brought their sorrows and perplexities. As wife and mother, she ordered well the ways of her household. As a friend, she was loyal, and much given to hospitality, and gifted with a peculiarly sweet and generous nature. Fulfilled to her was the promise, 'With long life will I satisfy thee,' for it was granted her to spend an honored old age in the homes of her daughter and son, and to see growing up around her children's children of the third and fourth generations.'

"The filial love and gratitude of children of such parents, as expressed in this window, we as a church will keep sacred while these walls endure.

"And now, to-day, we receive another deposit of this daughter's affection, another window, by which her great loving heart would perpetuate its tender esteem of her 'childhood's pastor,' the first minister of this church, Rev. John Watson Adams, D.D., who baptized Margaret Olivia Slocum and her brother, and received her into church membership."

The "Memorial of Love," which contains a copy of this sermon, gives the following description of these Memorial Windows and the inscriptions on them:

These large windows in the transepts of the church are the productions of Miss Mary Tillinghast, of New York. They represent the best work of the modern renaissance of the splendid art of the eleventh, twelfth and thirteenth centuries. In depth and richness of colors and jewelled effect, they recall the famous windows in the cathedral of Chatres.

The subject of the western window, erected by Mrs. Russell Sage and her brother, Joseph Slocum, to their father and mother, is the Heavenly Pilgrim. The Savior is pointing a sorrowing woman upward to the Holy City, which, in golden glory, breaks into view through the parted clouds. It is an inspiring illustration of the words, "In my Father's house are many mansions. I go to prepare a place for you."

The bordering panels are in striking harmony with the architecture of the church. With their rich jewelled symbols, they illustrate the twelve epochs in the life of the Savior. The following inscription is upon the base of the window:

> "To the Glory of God and in Loving Memory of Joseph Slocum, Trustee of the First Board of this Church, Born at Schaghticoke, Rensselaer Co., N. Y., July 19, 1795, Died March 30, 1863; And Margaret Pierson Jermain, his wife, born at Sag Harbor, L. I., March 4, 1804, Died July 19, 1891. This window is erected by their son, Joseph Jermain Slocum, and their daughter, Margaret Olivia Slocum, wife of Russell Sage."

In the eastern, the baptismal transept, Mrs. Russell Sage has now erected a second window, the creation of the same gifted artist. The Gothic canopies above enshrining the figures of Faith, Hope, Love and Prayer, and below containing the emblems of the baptism, and the side panels with medieval busts of the Apostles set in jewelled borders, very rich in color and leafage, are suggestive of the world-renowned Jasse window at Chartres. The central figures are life size; that of the Savior with uplifted face, expressive of a spirit of self-surrender and boundless love; that of the Baptist of rugged strength and prophetic inspiration.

The inscription on this window is as follows:

> "He who turneth many to righteousness shall shine as the Stars forever and ever. This window is presented by Mrs. Margaret Olivia Slocum Sage, in Memory of Rev. John Watson Adams, D.D., The Pastor of Her Childhood and First Pastor of the First Presbyterian Church, 1826 to 1850."

Col. Joseph Slocum, youngest child of Hon. Joseph and Margaret Pierson (Jermain) Slocum, was born in Syracuse, N. Y., June 24, 1833. He went to Cincinnati, Ohio, to reside in 1849, and there married Sallie L'Hommedieu, daughter of Stephen and Alma (Hammond) L'Hommedieu, son of Charles L'Hommedieu, son of Samuel, son of Sylvister, son of Benjamin L'Hommedieu of Rochelle, France and Southold, Long Island.

Soon after the breaking out of the Civil War, Mr. Slocum was commissioned Captain, and Commissary of Subsistence, and assigned to the command of General Ormsby M. Mitchell, as a member of his staff, and was engaged in active service in southern Tennessee and northern Alabama until that officer's removal to other quarters, and then acted as Post Commissary at Huntsville, Ala., continuing until ordered to Murfreesboro, Tenn. While on his way thither the train was thrown from the track by a Confederate scouting party and Capt. Slocum was severely injured. After his recovery he served on Gen. Horatio G. Wright's staff and was brevetted Major, and later was commissioned Colonel. He continued in service till 1867. In 1874 he moved to Chicago and three years later to New York City where he still resides (1908). He has one daughter and two sons.

Herbert Jermain Slocum, eldest son, born in Cincinnati, Ohio, April 25, 1855. Imbued with the spirit of his ancestor, the famous old Capt. Myles Standish of the Plymouth Colony, he entered the United States Military Academy at West Point in 1872, being appointed from the Second Congressional District of Ohio. He was a member of the Corps of Cadets which took part in the inauguration ceremonies of General Grant at the beginning of his second term as President of the United States.

He attended the Centennial Exhibition at Philadelphia as a member of the cadet graduating class in 1867. He was that year promoted Lieutenant and assigned to 7th U. S. Cavalry, and later served with his regiment in the Northwest. He participated in the campaign against the Nez Perces Indians and in 1880 was stationed at Fort Totten, Dakota Territory.

The official army record shows that on 22 June, 1876, he was made 2d Lieutenant, and assigned to 27th U. S. Infantry. Transferred to 7th Cavalry 28 July, 1876. 1st Lieutenant 22d Sept., 1883. Captain 26 Aug., 1896. Graduating at the Infantry and Cavalry School, 1883. Brevet 1st Lieutenant, 27th Feb., 1890 for gallant and meritorious service in action against Indians at Canon Creek, Montana, March 13, Sept. 1877. Major of I. G. Vols, 12 May, 1898. He took part in the Spanish American War, and was for some time stationed in Phillipine Islands and later on the island of Cuba where he rendered effective and important service under Gov. Magoon in the organization and instruction of the Rural Guard, which has achieved great success in preserving order throughout the island.

Major Stephen L'Hommedieu Slocum, youngest son of Col. Joseph, was born in Cincinnati, Ohio, Aug. 11, 1859. He was graduated at Charlier Institute, New York, in 1876, and soon after entered Columbia College. President Rutherford B. Hays having selected him for appointment to the Army on account of meritorious conduct as Aide on the staff of General Samuel D. Sturgis in the Indian campaign of 1878, he left college, and was assigned to the 18th U. S. Infantry as Lieutenant and ordered to Fort Assinibone, Montana, where he was stationed in 1880.

His official army record shows that he was appointed from New York 2nd Lieutenant 18th Infantry, 1st Sept., 1879. Transferred to 8th U. S. Cavalry, June, 1883. 1st Lieutenant, 28th Sept., 1889. Captain, 2nd March, 1899. Graduate of the Infantry and Cavalry School, 1883.

He has since been engaged in special and detached service of the Government. He is Military Attaché at the Court of St. Petersburg and Sweden, and has served in other important capacities requiring tact, wisdom, diplomacy, etc. He was sent to Africa on a secret and special mission which he accomplished to the entire satisfaction of the Government. He has shown on many occasions the courage and daring, as well as the tact, wisdom and quickness of action of the famous old warrior, Capt. Miles Standish from whom he is descended.

Lightning Source UK Ltd.
Milton Keynes UK
UKHW050748230120
357484UK00010B/941

9 789353 959333